# SANDBOX
## *to* MUSEUM

What to do when the faith you knew
doesn't work for you anymore

# SANDBOX *to* MUSEUM

JARED SCHOLZ

While a mass exodus of people have walked away from the Christian faith, those remaining in the Church are confused and frustrated, unable to understand how or why this is happening. While "deconstruction" is a real thing, it can sometimes fall on deaf ears as simply an excuse or a cultural trend that's being blamed for the decline. In this brilliant and highly engaging book, *Sandbox to Museum*, Jared Scholz articulates the concept of deconstruction in a way that helps the reader empathize with those who have deconstructed while also empowering the reader to engage and encourage those who are putting the pieces of their faith back together. Scholz gives cultural context to the deconstruction movement while also providing practical steps to move forward and grow whether you're the pastor, the parent, the peer, or the prodigal.

**BRANDON BOWERS**
Lead Pastor of Awaken Church and author of *Rise Above the Lies*

———

As a local church pastor, reading this book was at times like a kick in the shins, but it was also a window into a segment of our faith family that I have struggled to understand. Like Jared, this book is at times gritty, raw, and in your face. It is also an authentic, heartfelt invitation to those who have struggled to follow Jesus while embracing their church family. There are things said in this book that I did not like. But I'm glad I read it. The discomfort was worth it. Read it, and invite the Holy Spirit to speak to you as you do.

**CLINT SPRAGUE**
Lead Pastor of LifeMission Church and author of *Overflow*

*Sandbox to Museum* is an invitation to come alongside Jared and look deeply into an issue that doesn't just affect the church but our relationships with other believers and non-believers. With a tone that feels like an open-ended conversation, Jared uses humor that softens the harsh reality of our current culture. For a subject we may want to shy away from, he offers a practical guide to not only understand others better  but to look closely at elements of our own faith.

**SANDRA L. MARTIN**
Film Writer/Director

———

Jared has written an important book that deals with the reality of doubt and how to handle it.

Real relationships help us deal honestly with our thoughts, without the isolation the enemy seeks to create. Mature Christians seek to create environments where they are honest with their own doubts and allow others to help them work through them.

**JIM PUTMAN**
Senior Pastor of Real Life Ministries
and author of numerous books, including *DiscipleShift*

Cover design by Mackenna Cotten

Fedd Books
P.O. Box 341973
Austin, TX 78734

www.thefeddagency.com

Published in association with The Fedd Agency, Inc., a literary agency.

ISBN: 978-1-957616-41-4
eISBN: 978-1-957616-42-1
LCCN: 2023906858

Printed in the United States of America

For the brave souls
who engage yet again.

# Contents

Foreword      xi

Introduction      xv

**Part 1: WHY PEOPLE DECONSTRUCT**      **1**

    The Curse of Growth      2

    Hurts Hurt      17

    Racism Lurks      37

    Party Lines      40

    Hypocrisy      43

    Use Your Head      47

    Nominal      53

    Sus      57

    What You Gonna Do About It?      65

    Still Tribal      71

    Sin-thetic      80

    Bummer      86

    144,000 Problems      98

**Part 2: HOW TO AVOID THE COMMON PITFALLS OF
MODERN DECONSTRUCTION**      **129**

    Pitfall 1: Move fast.      132

    Pitfall 2: Harmonize.      141

    Pitfall 3: Do it alone.      155

    Pitfall 4: Live above scrutiny.      167

Pitfall 5: Skepticism is your superpower.                171

Pitfall 6: Ignore the reality.                          179

Pitfall 7: Reject all religion.                         181

**Part 3: WHAT WE CAN LEARN FROM THE
DECONSTRUCTION MOVEMENT**                                **189**

Death to know-it-all-ism                                192

Jesus à la carte.                                       196

Diversity Is Not a Four-Letter Word.                    200

When the Ketchup Grabs You                              203

But, why?                                               209

**Part 4: SOME CULTURAL FOOTINGS  OF MODERN
CHRISTIAN DECONSTRUCTION**                              **213**

Movers and Shakers                                      217

You're Good                                             223

My Truth                                                228

Check Yourself                                          234

In Dig Nation                                           236

Twins/Friends                                           243

Just You Wait, Buddy                                    246

**Part 5: HOW TO STOP THE BLEEDING:
A WAY FORWARD FOR YOU AND YOUR CHURCH**                 **249**

Acknowledgments                                         277

# Foreword

As Dallas Willard said in his classic book *The Divine Conspiracy*, we are blindly flying upside down. Our first attempt to gain altitude will end in certain disaster. Many of our traditional norms are being severely questioned or discarded entirely.

The current revolution is rooted in the relentless pursuit of the "authentic self" as described by Carl Trueman. This pursuit exerts great pressure on those who would embrace the revolution to cast aside all traditional moral limits, while resistance is met with bitter labeling and disregard.

The cry for things like racial, economic, social, and sexual revolution is growing in volume and often views people of faith with low confidence, especially as a potential source of good solutions. The teachings and principles of the Bible are seen as woefully out of touch and harshly oppressive. Scripture, in the eyes of some, is simply a tool in the hands of the oppressor.

When pastors and ministry leaders tragically and inexcusably fail, shockwaves batter the faithful. These failures wound many, exposing the vulnerable to abuse. These tragic failures sow seeds of bitterness, disappointment, unbelief, suspicion, and cynicism in the hearts of many. It makes sense that people of faith are tempted to question what they believe as the drumbeat of brokenness drones on unabated, too often traversing the center lane of the church. It is tempting to join the chorus of "Burn it all down!"

How should we go forward?

This book is an invitation to step into a safe space and examine our faith, before being swept along by the fast-moving modern current. Jared does not attempt to answer every question posed, nor does he pull us into the distracting weeds of high-level apologetics. He encourages us to pause and allow the suggestions found in this book to equip us to wisely wrestle with complexity.

I first met Jared Scholz in the summer of 2004. After adjusting to his creative fashion preferences and artistic mindset, he quickly won me over as we spent time together in prayer and laboring in Kingdom projects. He is a gifted musician, artist, creator, innovator, and skillful communicator. It has been a joy over these many years to walk together through a variety of circumstances and unique environments. He is a learner, a leader, and also a dear friend to me and many others. I trust Jared and you can too. Allow him to come alongside you in carefully examining the faith before you.

Yes, it is critical we all come to a point of truth because truth matters; it's a matter of life and death. There is reality. And, if any of us ignore it, we may pay a price that exceeds our imagination. Fully aware the stakes are high, Jared maintains a tone that seems to say, "Come inside, be safe, let's take this conversation to a different level. Let's not talk over each other, but truly connect."

The enemy of our souls continues to prowl as a lion seeking his prey. He employs his ancient strategy of isolation and lies. This book may be exactly what we need.

Steve Sizemore
Servants International

# Introduction

**The Scots about killed me.** We were averaging three hours a night of "sleep" in a crowded hostel, so yes, I was physically exhausted by the end of our ten-day mission trip, but they weren't helping things. I was near delusion, but beyond the physical toll, they just about killed my faith in them, and in Jesus.

My friends and I spent six consecutive years playing our songs on the streets of Edinburgh, Scotland, as the Fringe Festival raged on. Open-air rock and roll busking from America. Stars, stripes, and "accents"—I didn't have the nerve to tell them they were the ones who talked funny.

We had a system: catchy songs, mob dances, and our friends

meandering through the crowd with platters of warm chocolate chip cookies. It was like heaven on Earth, if heaven were to include stale beer, half-dressed performers, and an angry coffeeshop owner. But it worked! We sold copies of our music, built a following, made friends, and then invited them back to our rented flat for a house party.

On Monday night, we casually introduced a few acoustic worship songs back at our accommodation. Then at Tuesday's house party, our new friends were asking us to "play those songs that make us cry." In particular, they were asking us to sing the one about the spirit of adoption, and how God welcomes a broken humanity into relationship with Him. In total, I can recall four spontaneous confessions of faith that night alone: two in the cramped kitchen, and two on the couch.

Even I was shocked that our half-baked outreach worked. Kids got saved—now what?

I connected one of the new believers, Sonny, with a local pastor on the north side of the city. As the three of us met, Sonny barked through his lip-ring that the whole creation thing was a non-starter. I was deflated, but Pastor James was not.

"Well, you can follow Jesus and believe in evolution," the pastor said. His words echoed through what felt like miles of hollow culvert straight to my virgin and offended ears.

What?
He must be joking.

He wasn't.

Maybe that made *us* the joke? Had all of our effort and faith led us to entrust this spiritual infant to the care of a heretical pastor?

I was angry—more, I was scared, and not just for Sonny. I was panicky about how this affected me. Where would this type of talk lead us? What about Biblical authority? Did pastors even know what the Bible says anymore?

I still don't know all that Pastor James meant by this. Was he making room for an old-Earth creationist view? Or was it simpler? Maybe he was convinced that following Jesus starts with simply following Jesus. Maybe he was saying that Jesus would lovingly and graciously begin the work of heart and mind transformation at a pace Sonny could handle—in an order that Sonny could handle.

That feels familiar to me. If I had known from day one all that Jesus would reveal to and require of me over the years, I'd have sobbed with fear, but I also would have bought some steel-toed boots, because God's got a way of stepping on my toes—and dropping right hooks.

Pastor James's words were a right hook landing on this loose Midwestern pastor's chin. You see, I sat in that meeting bruised and tired. My spiritual questions and dissatisfactions had taken me extra rounds. I was dealing with my own spiritual turmoil. I had spent years quietly praying through my bravest mouthguard-stuffed lips. After all, the power is in the tongue, but I think I had bitten through mine, and it was bloodied and swelling.

At the time, I thought it was just a season—a season of doubt, and a season with big questions. But I was confident it wouldn't take long to find the corresponding big answers I was looking for. And it was a season, but I've come to discover that my faith lives on the equator; not much seasonal change there. In other words, my faith constantly wonders, mulls, and tests.

What I thought was a season has become a lifestyle for me.

I'm a questioner.

I'm endlessly curious.
And I'm always in need of some straightening out.

At the time, it felt like I only had two options:

Blind faith or all-out heathen.

Was I thinking more critically about my faith, or was my faith un-raveling? I knew the path to life was narrow, and up to this point, I was sure that just off the path, down in the ditches, there were evolutionists, democrats, and Calvinists—but I was starting to be less sure.

I was taking my faith apart like a LEGO house to see what it was made from. Today, we might say I was deconstructing. If I could have seen fifteen years down the road, I would have bought up all the "deconstruction" domains online and retired early. But I didn't, and now I work a lot.

Looking back, I'm grateful for the stress-testing of my faith—all the agitation of wondering, mulling, and testing. I think it's an age-old authentic and even necessary part of the faith journey.

I've encountered a cultural eye-roll in some Christian circles that seem to assume deconstructionist language is just a softer way of telling other Christians that you are walking away from the faith.

This most definitely is not my story.

Many of us are pulled into intense seasons of thinking more critically about our faith because we strongly desire purity. We want to purify our faith internally, and we also want to see the church, Christ's bride, purified.

I was thrust into this mess because I wanted to *keep* my faith, not because I wanted to leave it behind. There are still many who share this motivation.

For the sake of this book, we're going to speak of this intense faith season as *deconstruction*. Perhaps you'd like to think of it as old-school spiritual refinement, but we're going to go with deconstruction due to the cultural moment in which I'm writing. I've seen many others walk through this well. Like measured archaeologists, some have meticulously uncovered the dazzling, museum-worthy faith they hoped was buried somewhere deep.

Tiny brushes and great care.

Sadly, some others seem to have hastily quit following Jesus. They have demolished the faith of their youth, like a castle in a sandbox. The precious faith proves to be no match for their care-less toy truck.

Maybe you're articulating your doubts for the first time.
Maybe your friend is.
Maybe your kids are questioning and feel out of reach.
Maybe you're in church, maybe you've left, or maybe you run the church.

This book is for you.

My hope is to keep us from *Tonka-trucking* our faith.

Let's move from the sandbox to the museum.

I hope you'll see the complex conditions that grow faith.
I hope you'll see that authentic faith is destined to grow.

Faith is meant to purify.
Mature.
Sophisticate.

Here's some advice on how to do this well.

Here's some warning.

Here's some correction.

Here's some encouragement.

Here's an investment.

# 1 WHY PEOPLE DECONSTRUCT

# The Curse of Growth

**Some deconstruct because they feel like they've outgrown their faith.**

In the fifth chapter of his letter to the Hebrews, the writer slows down to weave together the Jewish high priest's work with the work of Jesus on the cross.

The blood.
The lamb.
The atonement.
Cleansing, it's all there.

It's rich and poetic and deeply theological.

The writer quickly shifts to directly address the reader, to plead with them to grow up spiritually. He says, "You don't catch on quickly. You should be teaching these things instead of asking for a refresher course. You're warming up your own formula bottle in the gas station between part-time jobs. You'd choke on a spiritual hotdog. It's embarrassing that you can't tell the difference between good and evil."

Based on your church circles, has Paul's rebuke lost its sting, or is it still relevant?
Has the church nursery been mislabeled as "sanctuary"?

Safe.
Kid-proofed.
Wired for entertainment.
And a strict no-cry policy.

Some people deconstruct because they feel like they've outgrown their faith. Perhaps they've looked around and everything suddenly feels so very childish. Their faith seems underdeveloped, simple, and not much different than hiding a tooth and waking up with a fiver under the pillow.

They might hear things like:

"Don't worry. Thunder is just God bowling."

"Well, I guess everything happens for a reason."

"God is in control."

But those anecdotes seem trite.

What if they're right?

What if they have actually outgrown their faith?

Like my son's lizard during shedding season, they've shed their faith because it just doesn't fit any longer. It seems quite possible that one might earn a PhD in biology yet still read their picture Bible.

Our faith must grow with us.

I'm concerned that, in an effort to see people reborn, and to bring those spiritual infants into the family of God, we have pared our faith offerings down to a kid's menu. One of the beauties of the gospel is that it is both simple and confounding. But the genius of God is that we move from a simple understanding to a more nuanced and sophisticated life of faith, one that is constantly expanding as the outworking of a simple gospel becomes more complex and significant.

With a napkin and pen, I could draw my family—stick figures to scale. But that's just an introduction. Come over tonight and I'll have the kids throw in a talent show between dinner and dessert. Cadence and Rilo will sing a duet that makes the birds jealous. It would be a much more robust experience than my sketch could ever provide.

What if my unbelieving neighbors aren't needing me to make the gospel simple as much as they are needing me to make it believable, sophisticated, and applicable?

Wherever certainty is synonymous with faith, you're sure to find those who outgrow it.

Faith is an invitation into mystery; faith requires we live with questions.

No questions.
No clarifying research.
Then there's no opportunity for faith.

And there are many faith communities where even a hint of doubt is sure to disqualify you from running the race. That brittle mold, cast in childhood, is destined to crack with any hint of growth. Maybe this goes without saying, but certainty and faith, while not mutually exclusive, are far from twins.

**The year of our LORD**, 2015 brought with it an exhilarating buzz to my hometown of Kansas City. The Kansas City Royals would go on to win the World Series! The team was young, but somehow, they were finding a new way to win each night. There were walk-off homers, fights, and nearly full stadiums, and I was in the stands to see it. It was actually worth the small loan I had to take out to pay for parking.

With all the winning came an interesting phenomenon. I was shocked by the number of 20-year-old girls who were suddenly and totally "way into" baseball. I never knew. My social media feed was suddenly flooded with friends in team tees, (still store creased), repping our hometown team for the first time ever, thick mascara lines under their eyes, and sporting the caption, "My boys in blue."

*My boys in blue.*

Possessive pronoun.
Note the *MY.*

With each inning of the game, I had the opportunity to observe one such fan in action a few rows in front of me. Her phone was documenting all the euphoria.

"Festive shoes on the seat in front of me" pic.

Nacho-eating pic.

Sunset pic.

Scoreboard pic.

She was here for it, and she wasn't alone.

The world wide web envied.


But something was off.


The timing.


She seemed to be a few beats late.

After the balk call, she wasn't the first to boo. Or the second. She joined the disapproving cheer once it was unanimous.

You see, a day at the "K" for her hit a bit different than it did for the golf-pencil-toting stat grandpa down the row.

She knew a home run was good.
Athleisure made her feel cute.

Friends laughing together was the draw.

These were her boys in blue! They were fun, strong, winning, and hers.

But she didn't seem to understand much about the game.

What's a balk?

RBIs?

She didn't know to hold her breath when the count was full. If she closed her eyes, she might not remember whether the player was batting left- or right-handed. While she was excited, she didn't know much about baseball.

Fast-forward a few years and the Royals have lost twice as many games as they've won. It's bad. And she's not there. When I think about her now, I imagine she is spending her Friday nights axe-throwing instead of cheering, and has sold all that blue gear online. I imagine she's come to realize just how shallow baseball is; after all, loads of excitement and camaraderie are great, but losing is a total bore. It just doesn't hold her interest like politics and anthropology class. After all, in this neck of the woods, gas station hot dogs are better, and she can park for free at her bestie's cookout.

Even the thought of the stadium is disappointing.

She's just not into the whole baseball thing anymore...

It might be said that she's walking away from a sport she never really knew. In case you're missing it, people are leaving a faith they never really knew, and they twitch when they drive by the church building. The fact is, it would be foolish for that former fan to look back and think she totally got it and she's just more refined than the rest—that everyone in the stadium was having the same simplistic experience she was.

"I mean baseball's fine for you, but I've kinda progressed."
It's a sentiment I've heard more than once.

Meanwhile, Grandpa Stats is still there, loving the complexity and smuggling in his own peanuts.

You see, outgrowing *your faith* is not the same thing as outgrowing *the faith*.

I ache for a world where Grandpa Stats tucks that short pencil into his hat, shimmies down the row, and shares the ins and outs of the game with whoever seems to be losing interest. That's called discipleship. I'm concerned that many outgrow their "boys in blue" World-Series-bound faith once the excitement dies and the crowd thins.

At the risk of mixing metaphors, I want to defend our girl from the ballpark. I might argue that many too harshly critique the Christian who has loads of passion and not much theology. I get that, especially long term, but there's something wise about a childlike faith.

Childish faith is not the same thing as childlike faith.

After all, it was Jesus who told us that we can't experience the Kingdom of God with a strictly grown-up posture. You must become like children to enter into it. I guess, considering those words, it's quite self-condemning to say that I've outgrown my faith.

I'm convinced that Yahweh will never promote you to a phase of life where you don't need to trust Him like a loving father.

May we grow in our childlike faith, not outgrow our childlike faith.

Trust gets a bad rap, but there's a lot of wisdom in trusting. You can't have faith without it. My youngest son nearly stepped on a heroin needle a few days ago. I took the opportunity to share with him my observations that heroin doesn't typically lead to a healthy or happy life. I found a few before-and-after pictures online and reiterated that there'll be no skateboarding if I find black tar in his backpack.

One child might say, "My dad told me smack is whack, so I'll pass on the party favor."

The next child might say, "I really need to find out for myself; pass the rubber tie-off."

When you think about it, wisdom can come from two primary places: a trusted source or personal experience. Dad or hard knocks. In some sense, it's great foolishness to have to learn for yourself all the time. From meth to porn, trusting the trustworthy is a far wiser path.

My favorite marriages and friendships to observe are those built on this sort of baseline trust.

"I trust my husband, so I don't need to rifle through his phone."

"I'm committed to this mission, so my boss doesn't feel the need to double-check my timecard."

"I'm not baking my son's graduation cake; my bestie told me he would handle it. He's reliable, so I'm not concerned."

Instead of saying, "I've outgrown the faith," perhaps it's more accurate to say, "I just didn't have enough faith for a life of faith." You see, a life of faith takes faith, and there's a data warehouse full of blogs to convince you that your faith is weak if it ever requires trust, or commitment, or reliance.

And if faith is about trust, there is no one more trustworthy than God.

My friend Pastor Clint has branded it onto my heart that to believe is to trust in, commit to, and rely upon. Turns out he's right. I'll never outgrow this hard truth. After a couple of decades of following Jesus, it has only intensified.

More trust.
More commitment.
More reliance.

It's fun-scary.

Like a full right-hand twist on our hand-me-down mini-bike throttle. Living a life of faith should always require some faith.

It's fun-scary.

There are Christian circles that are very uncomfortable with questions. If questions are not allowed, then having questions can often feel like it disqualifies you from the family of faith. Many who "outgrow" their faith come from this sort of environment. Sadly, these sorts of out-of-bounds questions have the potential to strengthen the faith of those daring enough to ask them.

If further study is frowned upon as faithless, then instead of reading a bit more, one simply leaves out the back door of faith. If cognitive dissonance is the secret sin of the "unfaithful," then one suffers in silence until they just can't do it anymore. A culture that bristles at this sort of reason and debate will never benefit from how it can deeply root a more scholastic follower—and the family of God needs scholastically-wired members.

The great Sho Baraka eloquently reminds us that,
"Life's a slam dunk when you're living with low goals."[1]

For pastors like me, the low goals of agreeable sermons and incessantly introductory-level theology can feel successful if all you're counting are how many new people have started attending the church. I'm certain that I have played a part in creating

1 "Ali," featuring Ali (CHE), Spotify, track 6 on Sho Baraka, Talented 10th, Lions & Liars Music, 2013.

a scholastically weak church culture. I've been more concerned about everyone understanding than I have been about tackling the difficulties of the text. I've brushed over complexities. I've given overly simplistic explanations. I've avoided whole fields of study.

As a church leader, I know what it's like to be low on study and high on performance.

Catechism yields to *At the Movies*.

Through the years, we've held seminars in our church that are deep dives into things like relationships, atonement theories, and Jesus' Jewish roots. If I'm not careful, I will discontinue these sorts of meetings because only a fraction of the church attends them, and of those attending, the amount of pushback and confusion is disproportionally high. All that to say, pastors will need to be reminded that these sorts of scholastic endeavors are worth it, and it might not hurt if, every so often, a church member encourages this sort of study too!

The body needs brains.

Christianity can handle the weight of your questions, study, and cognitive dissonance. Please don't assume that the answer you were given at the age of seven is the answer you'll be given at the age of twenty-seven. I say this based on experience. I've sat with a fair number of people who are dissatisfied with what they were taught as children but can't fathom the possibility that their children's ministry was meeting them where they were with age-appropriate teaching.

You can't assume that everyone shares your childish understanding. After all, just a few seats away, a man was bouncing his leg in anticipation because the guy on second was off the bag and had a low CS score. We understand this principle in academia. While most people might think it makes sense to schedule an hour with the chemistry professor to better understand the bond between carbon and hydrogen, they might also doubt there's any real value in meeting with the pastor to work through that Old Testament violence. Sadly, professors are more widely esteemed than spiritual leaders.

Some people are quite surprised to learn that their pastor has wrestled with many of the same questions they have, and even more surprised to hear of some of their pastor's more sophisticated conclusions.

Hand me the TUMS to get me through this podcast where some

23-year-old, angry ex-church kid thinks he could put C. S. Lewis in his place if he just had the chance. LORD, please resurrect Clive for just three hours, I'll get the popcorn.

# Hurts Hurt

**Some deconstruct because they've been hurt by the church.**

Nero was quite the angsty teen. He was a bit self-absorbed, violent, and all sexed up. "Kids will be kids," you might say, but he couldn't be sent to his room like your kids. He was the Roman emperor, adopted into the royal family and put in charge at about the age most of us get our driver's license. At this time, there was another rising star in the church. He, too, struggled with arrogance and violence, and he set out to write a letter to his young apprentice, Timothy, to guide him through the wild times of Nero's persecution.

In his second letter, the apostle Paul encourages Timothy to hold tight to what he'd been taught, because he *knew those from whom he had learned it*. Paul's appeal was that his words should carry weight because Timothy had seen Paul live out his own teachings. You can trust the teachings if they produce a healthy life in the teacher.

It's me encouraging my car-crazed son to save a good portion of his money as we drive around in the convertible Jaguar we paid for with cash. My point is that you know a tree by its fruit. And when a church community preaches a good message but doesn't have the fruit, people start to doubt the message. It's this very logic that leads some to quit following Jesus. The teachings of the church are often dismissed due to the character of the church.

Relationship advice from the school bully doesn't quite land.

Dating advice from a dirty old man is a bit out of tune.

Somewhere around 2006, our church was seeing a great number of new members coming from a church across town. Story after story left me jaw-dropped and disgusted. The pastors of the church were twisting scriptures something serious, like a coat hanger trying to unlock your car door.

The rationale went like this: men are in charge; women and children are to be controlled in order to honor God; children need discipline, and sometimes physical correction like spanking. Women are much like children; a godly man spanks his wife. If she still doesn't please him, he must seek spiritual reinforcement from his pastor.

And so dozens of women reported pulling down their pants to be paddled in the pastor's office.

It's agonizing to think of these dear women shifting from bruised cheek to bruised cheek during a Sunday morning sermon that most likely set the poor theological grounds for the abuse they were enduring. Ephesians 5:21 probably didn't make the preaching calendar cut, being that it speaks of *mutual* submission. The sermon probably didn't highlight the cultural setting of the original audience. It's my understanding that this bit of scripture was quite liberating for first-century women. The writer was lifting the heavy cultural weight of submitting to *all* men. We must see that the text is hoping to create a church culture of mutual submission to one another and to Christ, and foster a leadership tone of sacrificial love.

My guess is that the sermons in this church across town said nothing of Jesus' sacrificial love for His bride.

For those leaders, it probably sounded like quite the slippery slope to preach about sacrificial love. I wonder if they thought, *We just can't have that! Before long we'll have Christian men cooking their own meals and turning off their video games so the kids can get on YouTube after school, and it might lead to husbands feeling weird about hunting while ignoring much-needed maintenance on the house.* Male headship sounds a bit different when the authoritative man of the house is the leading example of sacrificial love.

Male headship is most celebrated in hell when a husband lives more like a brutal Nero than the sacrificial Son from Nazareth.

It takes great skill to detangle scripture from previous teachings and our current culture. It takes even greater skill to let the Word of God speak when it doesn't feed your strongest desires for power, comfort, control, and orgasm.

For those of us who have given our entire lives to the mission of Jesus, there's a deep frustration when we see the movement being hijacked by wicked people. With over 350,000 Christian churches in America, and an estimated 25 million Christian churches worldwide, these hijacking stories, like the one I just shared, hardly represent the majority of Christian leaders or church communities, thus making them even more discouraging for those of us who are committed to living it out day after day, year after year, neighborhood by neighborhood, and strength to strength.

Even so, flags can be idols, and the wrong people know this.
They know that they can unite people under the flag of a movement, even if they can't unite them under the values of the movement. The crusades were killing machines united under red cross flags.

Hitler preached his "positive Christianity" like the devil, and convinced great numbers of German church folk that Naziism was not anti-Christian. They literally flew a flag with a cross and a swastika. It was strategic: "Exploit their devotion to that flag for our own gain." If you find this hard to believe, then just research Hans Kerrl. He was the Nazi Minister for church affairs.

Minister.
Strategic?

The Nazi party convinced the great majority of those who worshiped a resurrected Jewish rabbi that the Jewish race needed to be eliminated.

Flags can be idols, and the wrong people know this.

For a great number of frustrated Christians, June 1, 2020, confirmed their suspicions that politicians still play their "gullible Christian base" by quoting scripture, holding Bibles, or hosting prayer breakfasts.

Please do not hear me saying more than I am.

Regardless of whose policies you agree with, I'm asking you to at least consider how this day impacted the already weary ones.

If you seek to understand why people are deconstructing, then you must hear me out.
Let's practice listening.
Quick to listen. Slow to speak. Slow to get angry.

I won't pretend to know all that went into President Trump's photo op in front of St. John's Episcopal Church in June of 2020. I hardly know what's in my heart sometimes, so I'd be a fool to think I know for sure what was in his heart that day. It grieves me, because it was a watershed moment for many deconstructing their faith.

He seemed to hold that Bible like a bachelor holds a newborn.

Awkward.
Unfamiliar.
Posed.

Books can be idols, and the wrong people know this.

Best I can tell, he was encouraged by his advisors to give a "law and order" speech in the Rose Garden and then walk to the church to pray, read a passage, or meet with clergy in response to the violent protests connected to George Floyd's death.

Said a different way, those closest to him suggested he humble himself in prayer, seek guidance from clergy, or offer hope by reading scripture.

It's reported that he chose not to pray, chose not to read scripture, chose not to meet with clergy, but chose instead to pose for a photo op in front of the church with Bible in hand.

I've seen no evidence of that Bible being opened.

It feels safe to say that most politicians will at different times employ a mis-handled scripture to curry favor from the Christians, like that time President Biden spoke of the palmist and not the psalmist. Palm, like that wild thing at the end of your arm.

Our aim in this section is to understand *why* people are deconstructing, and I've not heard of anyone leaving the church over Biden's gaffs, so even if it feels like a double standard, you don't have to agree with their assessment of the St. James photoshoot to appreciate that it was a dark day for the faith of numerous brothers and sisters.

But seriously extra credit for those who pause to at least entertain their premise.

Holy books can be idols, and the wrong people know this.

It's not just sinister outsiders commandeering symbols for their own gain, but much church abuse comes from the inside.

I'm numb to pastors caught loose-zippered in the park with their secretaries.

Sadly, it's just lost its surprise.

Whole cultures of abuse have been uncovered.
Sexual abuse of altar boys.
Sexual harassment of church interns.

One prominent Christian apologist was posthumously exposed for rape, trafficking, fraud, and many other abuses. So I get it.

It takes a miracle for many to see steeples as anything other than lightning rods, if indeed there does happen to be a holy and just God.

I hear and see a lot as a local pastor. I'm behind the scenes for all the infighting, unfiltered thoughts, and honest confessions. I try to be quite clear with people that, while I'm not a mandated reporter, my confidentiality is meant to facilitate honesty, healing, and justice. I will not offer you confidentiality to cover your sin or enable you to abuse at will.

I went to one of those "eat meat and weep" men camps one time. I didn't hate it for the most part. I got some time off, met some good men, and genuinely benefited from some intimate times with the LORD. I also learned the difference between an eagle and a buzzard—that was embarrassing. But to this day, I still get emotional when I think about the last day of camp. A teen boy was there with his father. The boy confessed to sexually abusing his little sister. For years.

What happened next haunts me.

The group nodded in hushed tones and congratulated him for his humility and vulnerability. Then his father hugged him and reminded him that this was all confidential.

I was furious.
I need a second just writing this.

A father just heard the heart-breaking news that his daughter has suffered at the hands of his son, and he turns a blind eye? This needs to change. I don't have the whole solution in mind, but what is clear to me is that we have a problem—a legal, wicked, festering, victim-wounding problem.

If you're a victim, I'm sorry.
I'll do my part to see Jesus' church purified.
I will not offer blanket immunity.

LORD, purify me.

LORD, purify our institutions.

LORD, purify our leaders.

LORD, purify our teachings.


The hurt is not just from sexual abuse; some hurts are from power abuse. Some leave the family of faith because they've been beat down by hotheads at the top.

I remember the first time I walked into a room and it went quiet. People started whispering, and one super-slick kid started shuffling his feet, inspecting the carpet, and whistling. Because I'm super tactful and reserved, I yelled, "When did I become that guy? Somebody in this room tell me when I became the 'we'd better behave around that guy' guy. . . . I'll wait!"

What was that? That was the pastor power differential. I don't like it, but it's real. I try to be super approachable, but even my best efforts can't erase the fact that I'm a pastor; in this case, I was their pastor.

Over the years, I've learned that a routine Thursday afternoon meeting is no news for me but can be anxiety-producing for others because they're talking to the pastor. I do appreciate being appreciated, but I have done all I can to serve our church alongside them, not over them. That said, there is an entire month in the new-school Christian calendar called Pastor Appreciation Month. Last year, I got one card. It was from Debbie, my mother-in-law.

The pastor power differential was highlighted in 2020 as our church tried to navigate the pandemic protocols. There were some families in the church who found it scary to talk with our leaders about how our COVID-19 responses were affecting them person-ally. They never emailed. Never called. No texts. No sitting in the back row with their arms folded. I learned a lot about the "power differential" anxiety of talking to church leaders.

The LORD used this moment to sharpen our messaging and en-couraged us to over-communicate, but more so, it was a reminder to be conscious of just how much courage it takes to stand up to perceived "power."

I've watched more than one documentary highlighting this pow-er abuse in churches. It's not uncommon for church cultures to dishonor the idea of honor by couching their pompous pride in ideas about honoring the *house* or honoring the *man of God*. This sort of thinking has empowered church leaders to pay a church intern $5 and a prayer for 16 hours of babysitting. That's power and privilege.

Power abuse can sound like this:

"How dare you email me about the sermon? That's the word of the Lord. Don't come against God's man."

"I don't care about your conscience. If your leader asks you to do it, then do it. Because delayed obedience is disobedience."

The reality is that the leader is often sinfully asking to live above accountability, and that's proven to be the recipe for disaster soup.

I've even heard stories that have an element of trafficking, as some pastors have threatened to use their connections to ruin a disgruntled employee's professional ecosystem if they quit. After all, a global denomination can be a small world.

We, the church, could really benefit from thinking critically about our internships, leadership paths, and volunteer relations. At the very least, a top-notch human resources department would do wonders. Okay, okay, we can call it the human resources ministry to get the board to pay for it!

My friend Dusti and I fumbled our way through one such

courageous conversation. We encountered both *power differential* and church hurt, as I was embarrassingly at the center of the problem. When Dusti was a teenager, I was her 26-year-old youth pastor. Now, sixteen years later, she and her family have started attending the church we pastor now. Recently, she pulled me aside to remind me of a conversation we had had all those years ago. At 14, Dusti had asked me how I felt about her marrying her new boyfriend while they were still in high school.

I winced as she recounted how I responded.

"You're a fool."

That's how I responded.
I called her a fool.

When she told me this, I immediately apologized for hurting her. "I would definitely have put that differently now. I'm so sorry." She hushed me to tell me that she was grateful and that, while it stung, it was great advice.

Dusti is the exception to the rule. Why? Because she spoke to me. I'm sure the next county over is littered with a few dozen former youth group kids with kids, who have never given me the chance to apologize for my arrogance or immaturity while I was their youth pastor.

Unfortunately, there are great numbers of people who will never have the nerve to start the conversation with those who have hurt them in the church. To be sure, many have simply moved on, but I'm certain there are some who have a hard time speaking to leaders because leaders can be perched in positions of power that feel scary to the one speaking *up*.

―――――――

I'd now like to transition to the hurt that seems to be thin-skinned— the type of hurt experienced when pride has been bruised. This is much different than the gender, racial, or power-differential hurt we've already touched on.

For lack of a better term, I'm going to call it "biased hurt."

In light of true abuses, it feels tone-deaf to lump them all together. There's a certain hurt that stems from a victim mentality, which I'll call the biased hurt.

James told me about his church hurt. He walked away from church and any pursuit of God because multiple Christian girls

had dumped him after realizing that he actually wasn't a follower. That's an example of biased church hurt, and an example of
wise women.

I've hurt many couples after explaining that I won't perform their
wedding unless one of them moves out. There's just something
unnerving for me about asking a Holy God to bless the union of
those who woke up between the same sheets just hours before.
You see, it's super easy to go to the courthouse, or get your college
buddy to get dot-com-ordained, but if you're asking me to stand up
at your wedding, you have to realize that this isn't just your big day.

It's also my big day.
It's the church's big day as well.

When I stand at a wedding, I'm there because I approve of the
union. I believe in the couple. In some strange way, my character is
at stake. It also speaks to my life's work as I talk about what marriage is, and as I celebrate purity, sacrificial love, and the Biblical
idea of covenant. As some sort of representative of the Christian
church, I draw a line for what marriage is, and what it is not.

If you want me, you get me full strength.

If you are hurt by this sort of standard, and you can't appreciate the fact that I must act with what I believe is integrity on your wedding day, that's biased. Of course, my participation in your wedding is something different than my commitment and support of your marriage, even if it began in a way that I don't support. If you lived together before you were married, then let's repent of that and move on. Grace upon grace.

Speaking of weddings, we had an incredible family leave the church because the facility's rental fee was too high for their wedding reception. That's biased.

In these sorts of conversations with people, I've tried to make a habit of clarifying what "church" hurt them. Not the name of the church, but I find it helpful to clarify whether we're talking about leaders or members? Organization or flock?

Is the church full of hypocrites, or is it full of imperfect people?

Are they saying one thing and doing another, or is there simply a difference between what they know is right, and what they find themselves doing? Perhaps many remain committed to the ideal while wading through the cesspool of their own missing of the mark, and that's actually courageous and loyal. When church folks sin, it takes a great deal of wisdom to know when it's a part of their maturing process or evidence of an abusive culture. I imagine we all initially favor one assumption over the other, but most likely it's always a bit of both.

For instance, those who grew up in abusive homes can still emerge with a strong conviction that healthy families play a vital role in society, even if they've never experienced it. It's like hating spiritual arrogance and at the same time acknowledging the prideful way I treated my brother at the men's retreat.

Some see this mismatch and leave. Some stick it out. The enduring church is built on the tears of those who simply stick it out. It's an attitude of *ride or die* with these imperfect people.

One famous pastor regrettably spoke of people getting run over by the metaphorical church bus. His idea was that either you get on or you get run over. This sort of corporate, "everyone is replaceable" mentality can be found in the church today.

**Some deconstruct because they have felt forgotten and uncared for by the church.**

As a friend, I have ignored others. As a pastor, I have forgotten the flock. As a person, I've been a jerk. As a weak man, I have been paralyzed with fear in times of crisis and have not cared for others when they needed it most.

I greatly admire my friends like Micah and Lance, who visit people in the hospital and stay right in the middle of the painful mess.

Sadly, difficult people have a difficult time staying in church. When you're always needing money or a ride or help in a crisis, church members can start to back up slowly because it's a lot of work meeting the needs of those who have a lot of them.

We, the church, give up too soon. We get distracted. We protect ourselves from the letdown by disengaging. We don't fight for relationships. And we have a hard time helping people follow Jesus in real time when their real time is messy.

We need more soup on doorsteps.
We need more hand-on-the- shoulder-in-the-frozen-aisle prayers.
We need more "just thinking about you" texts.
We need to help people move more often.
We need to take more time to listen in our Bible studies.
We need more May Day flowers, dinner parties,
and graduation cards.

My friend Michael told me about the meeting he had with his

pastor once he finally decided to leave the church. The pastor told him that this was going to be a really tough transition because Michael was going to lose all of his church friends.

My friend was shocked and skeptical.

The pastor was right. Far too often, we care that you're gone, but we don't care about you once you're gone. I'll admit there are some more nuanced reasons for this, but even still, we've got a long way to go in caring for one another.

**I am the chief of sinners.**

# Racism Lurks

**Some deconstruct in response to racism in the church.**

Jemar Tisby, in his book *The Color of Compromise,* tells of how the church underpinned slavery and racism as it bowed more to popular culture than the Kingdom's culture. One such occasion was in September of 1667 as Anglicans gathered in Virginia for their general assembly.[2]

For years prior, on the other side of the pond, the English Anglicans

2  Jemar Tisby, *The Color of Compromise* (Grand Rapids, MI: Zondervan, 2019).

had been required to free slaves who had accepted the gospel of Jesus and had been baptized. But here in America, the "need" for slave labor was much greater. Therefore, slave owners were working overtime to keep the gospel from their slaves so they wouldn't be forced to free them, since the church's policy said it was immoral to enslave a fellow believer. With such economic pressure on the line, chilling as it may seem, the church tailored its statute to deem baptism incapable of changing one's status as slave or free, thus making it acceptable to enslave Christians and non-Christians alike.

My close friend Brandon pastors a church on the East Coast. He told me a story that frustrated me and reminded me we still have a long way to go. A para-church leader in his city was working to get college athletes settled into churches in the area. As he brought them to a certain church, his white guests were treated much differently than his Black friends. White athletes were warmly welcomed, while the Black athletes could stand ignored in the middle of the church lobby. When the frustrated leader spoke to the pastor, the pastor replied, "You're absolutely right. We've got a race problem here. Thanks for speaking up. I'll continue to challenge our board and our members. It makes perfect sense for you to plug them in someplace else."

When we hear that Black brothers and sisters are still experiencing racial tension at church, it's easy to feel deflated and decide we don't want any part in this church thing.

From the paintings of blue-eyed Jesus to anti-Semitic theology, the stench of racism can't be covered up with a pair of air-fresheners in the church lobby. Martin Luther King, Jr.'s words from 1963 still ring true today: "Sunday morning is the most segregated time in America."

There's a great need for repentance and discipleship in this area. I couldn't begin to presume to know the exact way forward, but I do believe many of my Black friends would appreciate the opportunity to at least share their experiences in hopes that their Christian brothers and sisters would see and acknowledge that racial inequality still impacts our world.

# Party Lines

**Some deconstruct due to the politics of other church members.**

How could I bow my head when the head next to me was sporting a MAGA hat?

How could I raise my hands in worship when the hands next to me held a pro-choice banner last night?

Whether bricks or LEGOS, we all know it's easier to build walls with blocks. They're predictable, ridged, and uniform. If you've seen one, you've seen them all.

Unfortunately, culture loves blocks.

Voting blocks.
Special interest blocks.
Sexual orientation blocks.
Philosophical blocks.
Political blocks.
Evangelical blocks.
Progressive blocks.

After all, liberals are baby-killers, anarchists, and perverts.
And conservatives are racists, gun-lovers, and perverts.

I guess perversion is something we can all gag on.

Blocks are easily dismissed. Blocks deserve no conversation or clarifying questions. Blocks have no need for subtlety or understanding. To "do the work," I must quickly dismiss those I disagree with.

"I just can't..." has killed both neighboring and the local church's unity. The theme? We seem incapable of finding anything good in our challengers.

When was the last time you muted your earbuds to eavesdrop at the coffee shop only to hear, "Help me understand the basis for your vote. I would never want to misrepresent your perspective or assume the worst of you"? Cardiac arrest would be commonplace if this were ever to be normalized.

# Hypocrisy

**Some have left the church,
convinced that it's filled with hypocrisy.**

Not much has changed since Jesus' riff found in Matthew 23. It's easy to hear Him say, "Your hearts are far from God, but you're happy to offer the opening prayer for Congress, or have your testimonial aired on Christian radio."

The hardest part about being blind is that you can't see.

I have yet to meet a person who boasts about being a successful hypocrite. So often, I simply can't see my hypocrisy. My actions make sense to me. They are balanced. I give myself grace. I'm a work in progress, right? At the very least, the church would really benefit from at least hearing the critique. Whether it's the news story on the cheating pastor or simply the fact that the biggest gossip at work is the Christian guy, hypocrisy turns the cultural stomach like a gulp of clumpy milk.

Is it just me, or do people openly admit to serious character flaws and bad habits more than they used to? It's almost like our sin is accepted as long as we admit it—or find it funny.

"Yeah, my wife found my porn folder...haha."
"Sue me; I got a bit drunk and said some things to the college boys...haha."
"Players gonna play...haha."

In a world of casual disclosure, I wonder if the worst of all sins in our day and age is hypocrisy. We'd rather be seen as a loser, cheater, or scumbag than be exposed as a hypocrite. Maybe there is something here—an opportunity for the church to learn about confession; after all, that's out of our playbook, right?

Our church building sits on the main street of our college town. There are bars, concert venues, restaurants, hippy stores, one of those places where you pay them to lock you in a room, psychics, a brewing supply shop, a cat cafe next door, and us. On a regular basis, I clean our glass front door of spit, urine, angry lipstick messages that consistently start with an "F," full manifestos taped to the door, and even flyers for the latest satanic-chic gathering. The general theme is that the church is full of immoral people, doing immoral things, under immoral doctrines, led by immoral leaders.

No one is knocking the church door down asking how to be a good person. They assume there must be no "good and upright citizens" there, and that the church is morally bankrupt.

It seems clear that our city sees Christians as hypocrites.

I heard rumblings about the chicken sandwich across town. I ate it. I loved it. That chicken sandwich under-promised and over-delivered. And that's before I learned to double-sauce that bad boy. No one I know likes to feel duped or scammed, so when the church overpromises and under-delivers, people get hurt.

Hypocrisy does just this: overpromises character, and under-delivers righteousness.

I've been hesitant to buy that big ole "Welcome Home" banner all the cool churches have hanging in their foyers. I'm already needing a nap after lunch; creating a *home* is no small feat.

I once had a neighbor who spent his childhood participating in Bible-Bees and preaching classes. He was quite the model church kid. But he left the church in his late teen years after watching the head elder buy pornography and sneak off. You see, earlier that Sunday, this very same elder led the charge in having a sixteen-year-old girl stand before the church and apologize to them for her infidelity that would soon be made evident by her pregnancy. It's nearly impossible to commit your time, talent, and treasure to a place run by that guy.

# Use Your Head

**Some deconstruct because they've started thinking.**

If churches are like people, they naturally gravitate toward one of three primary worship styles: head, heart, or hands. There's great balance and maturity for the believer or church that utilizes all three, but one favorite seems to always try to take over.

I grew up in a *head* church culture. Long Bible studies. Baptism classes. Long nights in Daniel and Revelation. From my perspective, we mainly worshiped God with our heads, and I'm grateful for my scholastically minded formative years. However, if you weren't careful, you might think God could be fully known and conquered through sheer study.

Growing up, Christian maturity felt more like acing a Bible quiz than living in an ever-deepening, reconciled relationship with my Father God.

Imagine my surprise when my pseudo-uncle Joe carried teen-age me to the charismania-type church, and I was given the gift of interpretation of dance. They danced some mid-90s' Jewish-inspired dances, and I knew what they meant. They danced, and I could read their dance in English. That's some strange gift of in-terpretation stuff. I cried in worship and grew accustomed to peo-ple "giving words." Where I grew up, we *had words* with others; we didn't *give words* to others. That's where I learned to worship God with my *heart*.

While our church now continues to find ways to serve our city, the "social justice" church across town does it far better than we do. The impact they've had on our city is disproportional to their size and budget when compared to the other churches in town, includ-ing ours. They simply prioritize how the gospel should impact their *hands*! They *do* the work of the ministry, and our city is better for it!

My twenties and early thirties were spent in a couple of churches that I would call "charismatic-light." We loved God but left the snakes at the pet store. We danced at our seats, and while the aisles were free for rolling, I never personally saw that happen.

Churches like this are often brimming with passionate language. It could be argued that we sure did love Jesus, but in comparison to the church I grew up in, we didn't study God a whole lot. I could be wrong, but it seems to me that as a church staff, we struggled with the reality that too many in the church might have loved a God they only kind of knew. Just enough to *get saved*. Just enough to get excited. But perhaps we seemed to let the grittier stuff lie dormant more often than we should have.

Here's what I'm getting at: some streams seem to focus more on loving God than knowing God. So for many, once they graduate from youth ministry, they begin to study God for the first time.

They begin to study God for the first time.
Study, for the first time.

Some fall into this on their own, while some are shoved in by unbelieving coeds and professors.

They bump their heads.
It's all new.
They feel dumb.

And when there are no trusted spiritual mentors around to help them wade through some of this, their faith snaps.

Our Christian faith is meant to be stress-tested along the way, and the first round of it can be a real rip in the sail.

Alienating.
Disorienting.
Scary.

It's cold out there.
Reading Bibles in the fetal position.
It's quite the wake-up call to find out that the God you loved so much doesn't exist.

Wait a second, Jesus preached about hell?
Following Jesus will cost me everything?
There's more to the story than Christmas and Easter?

If He's so good, then why does evil exist?
A polygamist was a man after God's own heart?
What did you say about dinos?

We run out of reasons to love those we don't know all that well.

And when we have more *questions* about God's character than we have *understanding* about His character, the cognitive teeter-totter launches us into the park yoga circle, sixty feet east.

Our experience-based faith can easily cause us to make God in our image.

The New Age celebrity, author, and speaker Deepak Chopra, like a great Santa in the woods, stands with arms wide, ready to embrace every intellectually deconstructing novice. His pseudo-science has a way of tickling the intellect of bewildered Christians, especially if they haven't been challenged cognitively in matters of faith. So, when he encourages them to *redefine wrong*, it feels like they've been invited to a higher level of understanding. Now armed with two whole podcasts and a blog or three, they're ready to study and looking for a new home—as long as it's on a mountain, looking down on all those Christian simpletons from their past life.

Like, last summer *past life*.

I've noticed a common happening. Once buzzed from a little study, some fancy themselves scholars, and they study to find that there are intelligent truth-tellers outside of the Christian faith. Unfortunately, there's a church caricature that frames everyone out there as cave people. They don't know a thing. They wouldn't know a rock from a roll.

Deepak can be found saying something about keeping still on the inside when the world is buzzing around you. It's true. This speaks to the power of perspective, resolve, and hope. But I prefer the forty-sixth psalm, which speaks about trusting God when the waters foam, as well as being still and knowing that Yahweh is God.

You see, I marvel at a God who creates gravity much more than I marvel at Isaac Newton. It's one thing to recognize truth; it's quite another to initialize truth.

We can notice truth coming from many voices, but it doesn't erase the great difference between the author and the reader.

Creator / observer
King / paralegal
Musician / music critic
Christ / Chopra

# Nominal

**Some who deconstruct were nominal in faith and church.**

Imagine I spent the night at your house. Maybe I was in town to deliver a refrigerator I sold online and the Airbnb was just a tad too Airbnb-ish. Imagine you let me crash at your place. You showed me to my room and got me a fresh washcloth even though we both know I don't use washcloths. I'm more glide than lather.

Anyhow, you cooked, we ate, and the kids were side-splitting. I called home while you put your kids to bed. We had drinks on the porch, talked about old bands, went to bed, and I slipped out the front door to catch my 6:00 flight home.

Now imagine me blogging about how I was seeking legal separation and a name change from your household. Imagine me speaking as an expert about your house. Imagine if I led others to believe that I had the inside scoop and that there was nothing redeeming about your house.

The truth is, I wouldn't have the experience, knowledge, or tenure necessary for such pontification.

I wasn't there long enough.
I wasn't invested enough.

I didn't have the relational equity to understand what was actually happening within your home.

I was a nominal part of your family.
"Nominal" is a potent word.
It means "in name only."

It feels harsh and judgmental—and true.
If something is nominal, the price paid is very small compared to

its real value.

It's a steal.

For some, faith is a steal—an ill-gotten gain. It's a five-finger dis-counted identity.

Christian, in name only.

Nominal Christians invest very little time, thought, or treasure into their faith, and are surprised to not reap what they have not sown.

I find it hard to sympathize with the agitations of those who only went to a church service when there wasn't something better go-ing on. It can be quite underwhelming to read the farewell speech of someone leaving the spiritual family when in reality everyone knew they were more interested in the girls of Jesus than the gos-pel of Jesus.

Christian community must be seen as valuable. Christian commu-nity must cost its members if it's to hold any value at all.

You can't move out of a house you have never lived in.

I'm quite happy to know that there are unbelievers in the church, but I can't assume that an unbeliever has the perspective necessary to bring a reliable critique of the church, even if they tune into the live stream while Sunday shopping every single week without fail.

Christianity's wisdom is largely reserved for the enrolled.

Full submersion.
*Baptismo.*

One must enroll in a robust prayer life if they want to learn how to hear the voice of God.

Principles just won't cut it.

One must enroll in true sacrificial worship to see the wisdom and soul-shaping power of reconciliation spoken of in Matthew chapter 5. One must muscle through the inconvenience of dealing with people to truly enjoy God in the assembly—a pop quiz just won't do.

One must enroll in a life that helps them experience the rush of a friend coming to Christ in order to know that the joy of the LORD is their strength. Just singing the song falls flat.

# Sus

**Some deconstruction is the result of being unduly suspicious of organizations.**

There are toxic structures to be found in churches. There are leaders who are power-hungry. There are good ol' boys clubs, nepotism, and cultural norms that are soaked in pride.

A church can be organized in such a way that money is wasted, people are forgotten, and the business meeting is more celebrated than the prayer meeting.

So I get it when I hear someone say, in one way or another, "The bigger they are, the harder they fall." I can understand the anxiety attached to a leader gaining notoriety when you've seen power corrupt. It's an honest fear.

There are many unhealthy and highly organized churches, but organization is inherently neither good nor bad.

Rosa Parks organized, and so did the KKK.
Jesus organized, and so did Pontius Pilate.

If you're watching, you'll notice instances of overcorrection.
"Stick it to the man."
"I can't be a part of the machine."
"The whole industry is corrupt."

In the church world, there's incessant talk about wanting things to grow organically. If you haven't heard it, follow your nose to the patch-ou-li oil.

"Schedules are for the religious. If you're going to be full of the Holy Spirit, get rid of the clock."

"Let it flow."

"We should leave relationships to grow organically. Either they just happen or they're forced. And since we're all priests, we don't need pastors or collection plates because organization is bad."

It's curious to me that the most organic things I can think of grow in an organized manner.

Oak leaves look like oak leaves.

Dandelions pop their nasty little heads up, from the end of their nasty little dandelion stems, right on cue.

Tree roots fan out in a surprisingly predictable manner.

Church structure is best when it serves as a trellis. A trellis is built to support the weight of growth; it's a rigid skeleton to grow on. The church organizational chart must not be an oppressive exoskeleton that stifles, caps, and overbears.

Any hint of leadership or strategy in the church is triggering for some. One is irate that his Mexican pizza took 32 minutes in the drive-thru, but he's totally not into organized religion.

Taco Bell organization: good.
Church organization: evil.

One might demand to talk to the manager while doubting any need for a senior pastor.

Taco Bell leadership: *bueno*.
Church leadership: *espantoso*.

I hope your legs are in great shape if you're trying to outrun the need for organization and leadership in the church. It's shocking for some to find this reality even after leaving the church for the arms of the online deconstructionist community.

Follow me on this.

Some will get fed up with famous pastors. They pastor huge churches, typically have their picture on the front of their books, are mildly offensive on Twitter, and speak at the same ten conferences each year.

A great number of the faithful will leave the church and poke fun at its insider language.

"LORD we *just*…and *just*…so *just*…"
"Have you had your quiet time?"
"No, thanks. I don't want the church to lay hands on me, or love on me. Sounds creepy."

They're sick of the oppressive morals.
They find hypocrites.
They hate the "in or out" language.
They find insincere people going through the motions.
They fear getting kicked out.
They have secret reservations.
They poke fun at its sub-culture.

They find it suspicious that the church is unified by common experiences.
They see the church as grossly inbred.

"We've all had that camp high, right?"

"Did your parents argue all the way to church and then smile ear to ear for the greeters?"

Some run from the church to get away from those who are bound by a common story like, "Once I was lost, I'd be a mess without Jesus. Blah, blah, blah."

Imagine their surprise to find all the same realities in the deconstruction circles.

Insider language like "ex-vangelical, detangling scripture, and process theology." Celebrity leaders and gatekeepers like McClaren, Rohr, Webb, and others.

Deconstructionists have their own
morals
customs
fears
secret reservations
community
cultural norms

On and on.

There's a strain of deconstructionists who are united by common stories of abuse, loneliness, doubt, and a middle-school fury over purity rings.

Have you ever noticed that the amount of tension and conflict is much higher in threads than it is face to face? It might be good to question communities that work best online.

When I encounter what I call *reaction-based organizations*, I have to ask myself if they have built anything better.

How are their members' families holding up?
Is their mental health improving?
Does the city feel their benevolent impact?
Are they uniting people across ages, races, and social classes?
Are they growing in generosity and understanding of the holy?
Is the next generation starting where they left off, better off?

Is this a movement that could survive health, or does it need the fuel of dysfunction?

Does the incessant doubt wear on its membership?

Doing life together is hard, so my ears will perk when my eyes see the deconstructionist movement create a better community.

To put it plainly, online communities can't replace real-life community. I have yet to see a compelling example of real-life community centered around leaving the Christian faith.

# What You Gonna Do About It?

**Some deconstruct because they are frustrated by the way their brothers and sisters apply the scriptures.**

What good is faith and truth if it does not change the way we live? Inspiration must give birth to application. Our spiritual ancestors struggled, as we do, with the task of applying the truth to our everyday lives. They cut one another off over the issue of circumcision—sharp disagreement. They wouldn't rest until they had worked out all their sabbath-keeping laws. And Peter, for some baffling reason, was pig-headed about adding bacon to his diet.

Every generation is charged with the task of applying truth to their cultural context. Crop tops may or may not be a topic of discussion in my house. Styles change. Cultural tastes change. Modesty is heavily influenced by culture. Bathing suits were closer to suits a hundred years ago. Mullets used to carry different connotations.

Every generation gets some things right and some things wrong; my hope is that we continue to fail forward. The writers of the New Testament devoted a good deal of literary real estate to discouraging believers from sexual immorality. Maybe you've read the lists in Romans 1 or 1 Corinthians 6.

As our 1990s', totally buff youth pastors worked to contextualize the scriptures, some of their own lists emerged.

"Don't kiss till the wedding altar."
"You'll have incredible sex if you can get to your wedding night as virgins."

"Fill out this form detailing your sexual sins so we'll know how to better place you in ministry." (Translation: we don't want sexual predators in the kids' ministry.) Translation: perverts, in our eyes, are basically everyone other than denim-clad homeschool girls who field-trip to the nature preserve.

These well-meaning applications had far-reaching, unintended consequences. Due to the broad-brush approach, many victims of sexual abuse were convinced of their impurity and believed that their virginity had already been taken—so why try to live according to God's sexual ethic now?

There are countless stories of young people confessing their sexual sin to the local youth pastor or internship leader, only to learn that their sin was simply unpardonable, and they were asked to leave the church.

While purity rings were placed on girls' fingers as a reminder to "save themselves for marriage," being asked by your youth leader to take it off when you're caught fooling around at the lock-in caused a great deal of condemnation that only distanced many from the heavenly Father they longed to know.

Decent ideas, but an indecent exposure of one's sexual mistakes.

We must take great care not to mistake our harsh, self-righteous moralism for tough love. Standards and expectations are fruitful, but gentleness is still a fruit of the Spirit.

Grace and truth.

Spirit and law.

Truth in love.

While some are able to look back and see where well-meaning people made mistakes, others cannot see past the hurt.

Some are able to detangle the godly principle from the man-made standards, while some are not.

As a '90s youth group kid, I'm here to testify that rigid, man-made applications have cost me a good number of compact discs, as we shattered them and cast them into the rolling trashcan of Hades, stage left, only to repurchase them digitally ten years later.

Ideas have consequences, intended and unintended. We must all lean into this complex tension.

It takes thick skin and a soft heart to wade through it all.

Luke preserved the early church's growing pains for us in the sixth chapter of Acts. The church was running a soup kitchen as well as holding church services. Some widows were going hungry, while others were shown to the front of the line for second helpings. My assumption from the text is that they needed more hands, or more oversight down at the mess hall, so they asked the preaching pastors to pick up some extra shifts.

Now, how were they going to apply God's vision to their everyday schedules? On the one hand, they needed to meet the needs of the poor, and on the other hand, the church needed to grow in wisdom. The budding church needed to be corrected, trained in righteousness, and equipped for more good works, and teaching was to play a big role in all of it.

People need both food and sermons—the same is true today.

So the prevailing question is one of application: "Okay, since this is true, what do I do now, and how must I respond?"

How should I vote?

Should I take a vow of pacifism and dodge the draft if it were to ever occur again?

Do I yell or whisper?

It's a difficult line to toe as a disciple, pastor, local church, or denomination. How often should we instruct people on what to do? How often should we leave the application open-ended in order to empower people to set their own biblically informed boundaries and determine their own biblically informed values?

When we try to apply the scriptures, "voting your values" is no easy task.

I must say that threatening to leave a church because you don't like their extra-biblical application, only to demand that they fix the problem by applying the opposite extra-biblical standard, seems dishonest. Either the church has the freedom to apply, or it doesn't.

# Still Tribal

**Some deconstruct as they look for a community**
**they want to belong to.**

I will agree with those who say our culture celebrates the individual, but most of us tend to find the bulk of our identity through
belonging. And that most clearly happens in our community of
friends.

Think this through with me.

Tribes of Israel

National pride

Race

College majors

Greek houses

Preppy

Punk

Artists

High-school cliques

LGBTQ+

Sports fans

New moms

Now imagine with me that, for a plethora of reasons, one feels out of place at church. They have secret reservations, theological questions, personal insecurities, or they just simply have big feelings about how they'd do things differently.

They incessantly think,
*These are not my people.*
*I do not belong here.*
*I'm simply looking in on something I know nothing about.*

Now imagine that in the privacy of their own online search, they find a group of people just like themselves, an entire thread of people who never closed their eyes while singing, or put their purses down at church, because they just couldn't get comfortable.

Some find the back door of the church because they were never comfortable in its living room, porch, or kitchen. They never felt like they belonged. So they were never themselves.

I stumbled upon a provocative podcast called *Meaning in the Middle*, wherein Ryan Adams and Landon Pontius spar over big topics. One is living as a follower of Jesus, while the other deconstructed into agnosticism. One particular episode highlighted some things about belonging that I'd like to share with you.

Pontius and Adams say that the fastest way to belong is through the dark emotions of outrage, suspicion, or traumatic experiences. They went on to share that, on average, it takes about three seconds to form a bond over a negative experience, but approximately 30 seconds to form a bond around a positive experience.

There's an immediate therapeutic pay-off to finding your misfits, at least initially. But over time, there seems to be a yearning in the human spirit to connect over something more than just shared traumatic experiences.

I told my friend Lance that I felt like the shelf-life of bonding over disgust was short. I told him that I thought it starts to feel icky quite quickly. He brought forth a great point: "I wish this were more true, but I am concerned that some systems have gotten very good at creating new boogeymen/things to be disgusted by, deepening the bonds over time to the point of unquestioned allegiance."

But even still, Ponzi schemes only work when there are new victims in the hopper. It's trickle-up economics, and given that outrage has a shelf-life, some pockets of internet communities must maintain an abnormally large front door to stay viable.

In my very limited view, the ex-vangelical community can begin to feel more like the local VFW bar than a VA hospital. The hospital acknowledges the wound and seeks healing. But in many instances, the VFW bar is a hideout where you swap war stories, compare scars, numb pain, and bond over shared enemies. It's where you create community outside the home while running from the overbearing responsibilities of living with the family you have there.

Perpetual irritation breaks down the human soul.

Heart problems, stroke, weakened immune systems, anxiety, depression, suppressed lung function, shorter life spans, weight gain, and relational rigidity are all symptoms of this constant indignation.

Relational rigidity?

I had never heard of *relational rigidity* prior to researching for this book, but I've seen it play out more times than I would like. Relational rigidity identifies the internal habit of expecting friction and rejection from *every relationship* at some point. It says that it's just a matter of time before each and every relationship fizzles out or blows up.

I'm concerned that in our culture today, far too many people are becoming relationally brittle. It's becoming less common for people to have friends who disagree with them. These days, disagreement is interpreted as rejection and undermines a sense of belonging.

This need and longing to belong to a people works itself out in another powerful way. We want to change our name and move to the coast when our family goes nuts. Given that our identity is thoroughly formed in relation to our associations, many have distanced themselves from the evangelicals, or fundamentalists, or morally depraved fallen pastors on the news, doing all they can so as not to be seen as "one of them."

To be sure, bonding over faith, friendship, or a higher calling is the most fruitful bond for both the individual and the community, but this takes time. We must fight for relationship. We must swallow our pride. We must say hard things. We must listen to hard things. We must be willing to disagree in love.

Church community costs the individual a lot, but I'm not alone in liking expensive things.

The *Meaning in the Middle* podcast also put some language to something I'd been pondering for some time, about how to know if your hurt is biased or not.

I've gotten wound up a time or two into the flurry of showing battle scars. I have exaggerated or reframed my story to be a bit juicier. Before long, it was me against the cartel, when in reality, I got two snarky emails. I've also been encouraged on more than one occasion to view my past through a new lens that made me look better, and made those other people look worse. Some people just have a way of spinning every situation and training everyone around them to do the same.

Simply put, some of us need help figuring out whether we have truly been abused by the church or not. WebMD isn't gonna cut it.

Adams says, "You can't heal from a wound that isn't yours. It cheapens the experiences of real abuse. And an imported story-line should never replace or circumvent personal introspection."

This personal introspection is important. It's hard work to truly dig into your own story. It's hard to maintain a humble heart that can see where you went wrong. It takes some real Christlike love to give your enemy the benefit of the doubt, especially when you have been mistreated by others. It's not an all-or-nothing verdict, and that sorting is hard work.

It's hard to tell the truth when your new friends hand you a storyline that puffs you up.
Even if it's not exactly true.

Take notice: anytime someone tells you how you should feel about something, manipulation is afoot.

Imported storylines are tempting for everyone involved.

"We've all experienced abuse, right?"

"That pastor is one hundred percent a narcissist, right?"

"We all feel the same way about that, right?"

And to be fair, there are plenty of imported storylines in defense of the church too.

"Ah, people who leave the church are bitter for no apparent reason. They just need to grow up, right?"

"Deconstruction is a fancy word for doubt, right?"

There's a great temptation to skip to the *what* while skipping over the *why*. In parenting, it sounds like, "Because I said so." In Bible study it's, "Because that's what *we* believe."

Now, there are moments when the wisest thing to do is obey before understanding, like when we are told, "Don't touch the stove." But our faith must incorporate deeper understanding and complexity as we mature.

Speaking of maturity, here's a curious observation. Some of my friends are turned off by the church's apparent practice of asking people to sign off on a list of beliefs, regardless of whether they understand *why* we believe those things or not. But these very same people are quick to sign off, *carte blanche*, on any story that indicts the church. It seems a bit unfair to say, "Don't sign off on any sweeping statements *from* the church; now sign off on all my sweeping reports *about* the church."

On my best day, I refuse to demonize the thing I'm leaving. On my best day, I can recognize my "breakup feelings" and not overreact. It's a real struggle for most of us to distance ourselves from the church without nitpicking it.

# Sin-thetic

**Some deconstruct as they reject an inadequate, weak, or weird version of faith.**

I used to think I wasn't a fan of juice. I'd tried orange juice, apple juice, and no less than 632 fruit juice cocktails involving cranberries. Cranberries are the Kevin Bacon of the juice world.

And then I ran some fruit through the mystery machine stored in my garage that my friend Jake gave me. What was this nectar of heaven? Maybe it was just the natural sugars, or the almost magical experience of "solid fruit in, aromatic juice out," but I was giddy.

Before I knew it, I was a week in, frolicking around the kitchen island, a drink in each hand, celery approved, bananas banned, and I was broke—juicing is a rich man's game.

You see, up to this point, I had only had juice in hotel lobbies, out of those three bay machines with the rubber straws dispensing liquid like the giraffe tongue in my selfie at the zoo. That juice is built differently. In my experience, that juice is a bit off. It's either weak or weird. Either you get a water-ish swig or an oily experience that coats the roof of your mouth—barely edible wax, too sweet, and too strong, almost like it's trying too hard, popping its collar, bouncing on its toes, saying, "I'm cool; I'm juice. Who's asking?"

But it was a fake, an imposter.

Have you ever thought:
*There has to be more than this.*
*This doesn't feel like the whole story.*
*This doesn't feel wide enough, deep enough, or tall enough.*
*Something feels off.*

The Christian heritage is full of people in this restless condition.

Martin Luther gave us at least ninety-five reasons to reject the weak, man-made faith of his day.

Dietrich Bonhoeffer, the German pastor, prophet, martyr, and spy, worked to put Jesus at the center of protestant churches as the Nazis worked to unite them with Hitler at the center. It's too weak to trust in a man. It's too weak to battle flesh and blood. It's too weak to wring our hands instead of folding them in prayer.

Paul rejected a faith that held hands with the customs of his day. He called the church to a strange purity in the face of persecution.

Job rejected the sensible yet demonic theology of his friends and has been a great source of strength to bewildered Christians to this day. Who needs enemies when you have a friend like Bildad? Bildad was convinced that Job's suffering was unquestioningly due to his secret sin, and that his kids would still be alive if they hadn't been shameful as well.

I wouldn't be surprised to see him turning tables at Hobby Lobby at the sight of one more encouraging verse quoted out of context and painted on a perfectly distressed piece of plastic barn wood.

C. S. Lewis had a way of melting all the nails in the house of faith, and slowly walking through the rubble with a smile on the corner of his lip, a cup of tea in his hand, child-sized wire glasses on his nose, and a threatening pen in his other hand. He called out superstition. He elevated the value of debate. He sought to understand reality, and reality led him to place his faith in Jesus. Rationality was legal again, and he blurred the lines between the secular and the spiritual in a way that felt like a real ripping of the veil for the believers of his day.

Jesus of Nazareth leveled up the faith of His day. He didn't come to pour out the cup of the law; He came to fill it to overflowing. Outward policies were too weak; He critiqued hearts and motives. Women and children were celebrated as fully functioning people of faith and the focus of His Father's affection. Jesus not only rejected weak faith, He denounced weird faith. You know, that faith that feels synthetic, the stuff that coats the roof of your mouth? That faith that feels put on, like edible wax? That faith that sounds like it's trying too hard? Too strong. Too sweet. That faith that waxes poetic, but has no real vitamins?

The revivalist Wesley brothers, and their friend Whitfield, sought to make disciples in a day and age when mere church attendance was an acceptable result of following Jesus. The Methodist Church created a reproducible process for helping people follow Jesus in real time. They administrated to the glory of God. They added methodical disciplines to the discipleship journey, and the forever Kingdom will be more fun because of it.

Chances are your church seeks to reject weak, fake-juice faith in one way or another.

We're not alone in this endeavor.
There's a long line of spiritual ancestors who tasted and saw.

Our generation's weak faith sounds more like the American dream than the self-sacrificing gospel of Jesus.

Yahweh asks His people to give up their rights and to notice and serve their neighbors.

But too often we demand our rights and serve our neighbors notice.

In my imagination, weak faith looks like me on October 31, 1989. I wanted to be a football player for Halloween, or for the Christian kid, the *harvest party*. My mom made it happen because she can make anything happen. She stuffed one leg of a pair of panty-hose with towels, draped the mummy leg over my shoulders, and popped the jersey over top. She then smudged mascara on my cheekbones and sent me to school. Imagine the letdown when my classmates patted my shoulders only to create a dust cloud and a thud, as opposed to that rigid clack of actual football pads.

Weak faith stands in its oversized helmet to speak with youthful, bombastic certainty about creation, the flood, atonement, hell, the afterlife, the state of the dead, and every bit of minutia in between.

At some point, those brave faces fall, discouraged. They just can't honestly reach a place of certainty around these open-handed beliefs. I'm concerned about the amount of pressure we put on people to be absolutely ready for game day.

We need more debate-style nights up at the church. Dim the lights. Gather in a circle. Heck, I'd volunteer to vacuum if you need that Texas Roadhouse peanut policy to make it go.

So where do we go to learn, disagree, get fired up, and end the night with a hug? I'm talking about a really tight hug. A hug to release the lingering frustration and underscore our commitment to the other person and our commitment to the unity of the church.

I long for this type of gathering.
I did it once in my living room.
A few left the church.


Anyway...

# Bummer

**Some deconstruct because they're disappointed.**

The Miami skyline updated in a matter of seconds in June of 2021. After years of neglect and rust, all twelve stories of the Champlain Towers South simply collapsed, like a wedding cake slumping in the summer sun. Ninety-eight people were lost. Condo upon condo, it was all gone. I must admit, I've never given much thought to the integrity of public buildings. I mean, bathrooms? Yes. Footings? No.

We were vacationing in Miami at the time of the collapse. Some days later, a very curious thing happened. Motorcycle after motorcycle passed us, headed in the opposite direction on the highway. They were police motorcycles—dozens of them. Oncoming traffic got eerily quiet. Police. Silence. Then Escalades with flashing lights and armored vehicles, coming down the highway like geese in a V formation. The president was in town to bring comfort and leadership to the people of Miami in their time of shock and grief.

A few months later, I would have my second brush with President Biden. A pandemic shutdown and a hotel mix-up landed my wife, Mandy, and me in a swanky hotel in Manhattan. Our lobby was filled with suits and foreign languages. There were alligator suitcases, bedazzled face masks, and lots of men whispering into their shirt sleeves. Over the course of two days, municipal vehicles lined up bumper to bumper outside our hotel and the surrounding buildings. Salt trucks, garbage trucks, dump trucks were all literally bumper touching bumper, forming a crude anti-bomb barricade. Police were on every corner, and things felt alert yet secure. As it turned out, the 76th General Assembly of the United Nations was happening across the street, and we were in the same hotel as a great number of foreign diplomats. Poland was there. Egypt was there. France. Iran. And President Joe Biden. Again, there was the motorcade, helicopters. and suits—lots of suits—plus a handful of pantsuits.

What does a motorcade like this cost?

$2,614 per minute.

$1.2 million per day.

Motorcades are nothing new. They're ancient.

About 700 years before Jesus, the prophet Isaiah spoke of what it takes to accommodate a king's travel. If you can, envision with me a world before the Department of Transportation and asphalt. Okay, so now that we all have Missouri in mind, if a king on wooden wheels needs to go out of town, it's going to take some work. Winding roads need to be straightened. Holes need to be filled. Valleys need to be raised. Hills need to be shaved. We'll need to deal with steep drop-offs, highway bandits, and rocky passes.

About 200 years later, the prophet Zechariah would prime the hearts of God's people by talking about a king coming to town who was righteous and could save them. Imagine the bated collective breath as they envisioned a world without wicked leaders—a world where they were the winning team.

This was the backdrop of Palm Sunday.

When Jesus came in, they hardly noticed that His transportation was a compact rental from that weird company a few miles from the airport.

It was still euphoric.

There was singing and the waving of palm branches.

It was supernatural.

"Blessed is He who comes in the Name of the LORD," people shouted. "Hosannah! Hosannah! Hosannah!"

And then Jesus was murdered five days later.

Great disappointment.

Disappointment is a part of the human experience.

You've sung the bridge to "King of My Heart" a thousand times and then God didn't come through for that healing. You went to the mission field and the harvest was not plentiful. You pared down your wardrobe to accommodate that prayer closet thing, markers on the wall and everything, just in time for God to go silent.

It takes some hard-earned *equilibrial agility* to manage expectations with God.

Yes, I made that phrase up.
*Equilibrial agility*

Have you ever seen one of those inflatable punching bags? My favorite is the Bozo Bop Bag. It looks like a clown with a target on its chest. It has some sort of weighted disk or sand or something in the bottom.

Hit it with a right jab and it pops back up.
Hit it with a left hook and it pops back up.
Throw a kick to the red nose and it pops back up.

The Bozo Bop Bag has equilibrial agility.

It quickly and consistently adjusts to being knocked off balance. It's crucial that you develop equilibrial agility in order to manage your relationship with God.

Is He letting you down or delaying gratification?
Is He silent or are you deaf?

Has He forsaken you or is He crying in the corner as He fights the urge to intervene? Does His being in the corner necessarily mean He has forsaken you? Is your suffering, in some Christlike way, going to help others find freedom?

Do you see Jesus as *your way to* truth and life or is He *the way*, the truth, and the life?

*Equilibrial agility*

We need some Bozo Bop Bag faith.

I wonder if we get knocked down because we don't understand the true gospel. I wonder if we tend to add to the gospel because the gospel feels too bland. It grants no promise of success, no promise of ease, no promise of understanding it all.

Perhaps we're high on *prosperity* and low on *gospel*.

We must admit that some reject the gospel because they are slaves to sin, not because the gospel ain't worth responding to.

I wonder if we do a bit too much selling and not enough proclaiming.

Could it be that a great number of people are knocked down and dragged out of the great race because they were sold on some man-made promises that were loosely tied to the gospel and those promises simply didn't materialize? And we sure do love that material, don't we?

Getting fired feels like a blow to the gospel, but the gospel never promised me job security.

It would be disorienting for God to call me to celibacy, but the gospel never promised me an orgasm.

It feels like a punch to the gut when someone speaks in tongues, but the gospel never promised that I would understand everything.

The gospel does not promise us personal satisfaction, perfect clarity, healthy relationships, or financial success.

At the end of the day, there's a lot of wisdom in pursuing those who disappoint you, even when it's God. Just because I'm disappointed doesn't mean they disappointed me. Nor does it mean that they're a disappointment.

Somebody once told me that if my gospel didn't work for the impoverished single mother in Africa, it wasn't the gospel. That's stuck with me.

I appreciate Pastor Ray Ortlund Jr.'s straightforward approach to the gospel.

*I'm a complete idiot.*

*My future is incredibly bright.*

*Anybody can get in on this.*

All right, I'll take a shot at the gospel.

The good news of Jesus is "Get in here."

The culture of heaven is available to everyone, everywhere, right now, so get in here!

Seek His face.

Walk in His ways.

Live in His family.

Connect to His body.

Jesus' life, death, and resurrection reconciles us to Yahweh.

Living in this Kingdom saves us, changes us, and puts us on mission with Him.

We might add to or try to improve on the gospel, but whether we're adding to it or taking from it, we lose our balance.

I have friends who have gotten ultra-excited about one element of the faith, and then made it their *only* element of faith. They've gotten out of balance, and when all your weight is on one leg and your spiritual knee gives out, you're done for. You're disappointed by God.

For instance, if we live on *intimacy* with the Holy Spirit alone, we can't handle the disappointment of not *feeling* Him.

If we see miraculous healing as the only possibility for the faithful, then we can't handle the disappointment of a friend dying of leukemia.

If you think that the apex of living for God is prayer and worship, then you might log hours in a prayer room but never learn to love your city or raise your kids. You'll likely be left with a deep-seated disappointment in getting a job because it pulls you away from your 24-hour *highest calling* of praise and worship.

Imbalance can lead to great disappointment.

Disappointment gets a bad rap.

Disappointment might be the most fruitful emotion humanity experiences.

In the early years of our church, my mentor and fellow church leader, Steve, told me that he was unhappy with our small group. If my trauma remembers right, he said, "This isn't what I signed up for." It was jarring news to be sure. He continued, "There's a bottleneck at the drinks. We need to move the drinks to the end of the food line so that people don't have to cross traffic near the refrigerator. And that's not all. The kids are too loud in the basement. We need to move the discussion group up one more floor."

He was disappointed.

Can I tell you that the very next meeting, we moved those drink cups and we pulled the dining room chairs into the upper living room? And there he sat, happy as a peach. Steve's disappointment led to growth, and not to overstate it, but it has probably led to years of more fruitful discipleship. We've found it easier to help people follow Jesus in real time, with less frustration and more quiet moments.

Pig slop for dinner was disappointing for the prodigal son, so he turned toward home.

My friend Mike got fed up and started working the steps in AA.

Imagine the disappointment the disciples had to shake to carry on the mission of Jesus without Him in the flesh.

Like the practice of ironwork, it seems to me that disappointment needs the water bath of community. Have you ever seen a blacksmith, with gloved hands and a huge pair of tongs, dip a glowing red piece of metal into a bucket of water to cool it? We need the church small group to help us absorb the disappointing sting of a diagnosis. We need a scholastic Bible study to help us deal with what seems like an Old Testament approval of polygamy.

Paul tells us in his second letter to the church in Corinth that God uses sorrow to lead us to repentance.

May the LORD get His full reward as we are disappointed by our prejudice. May we be disappointed with our shallow theology. May we be disappointed by our coldness towards the poor. May we be disappointed by the absence of prophesy and intimacy with the Holy Spirt. May we be disappointed by the moral failings of our leaders and co-laborers.

I long for an all-consuming wave of righteous disappointment to consume every expression of Christ's church, that it might cause us to return to our first love.

# 144,000 Problems

**Many deconstruct because they have Bible problems.**

Contrary to popular opinion, the majority of Christian churches still read the Bible. The Christian faith comes from a long line of people who have gathered around agreed-upon oral or written works and worshiped through their study and application.

*Sola scriptura.*
Scripture alone.
They didn't really mean it though.

It's always been more *sola scriptura* (plus reasoned debate, the work of the Spirit to interpret, contextualization, and re-contextualization, all in order to apply it to the current times, preach it, and teach it).

I so resonate with the party favorite phrase "The Bible says it. I believe it. That settles it!" But I have yet to meet a person who's used that phrase who takes the Bible at face value. I have yet to find a faithful reading of the text that doesn't acknowledge hyperbole. Poems are to be read as poems. Parables are to be read as parables. Ceremonial laws are not moral laws. One must try to understand how the first audience would have heard what was being spoken. And it's going to take a work of the Spirit to help me detangle scripture from my own cultural leanings.

Mark 2 is a great example of both entanglement and humility. In the King James Version, we are told not to put new wine into old bottles, because the bottles will break. It just didn't hit like it should. Glass itself doesn't expand, but instead, the cork creates the expansion capability for the pressure of the gas being created during the fermentation process. So why would an old bottle burst with new wine?

First-century Jews poured wine into leather bags. As the wine fermented, the leather stretched to capacity. If someone were to place grape juice into a pre-stretched old satchel, then as the juice turned the corner to adult beverage, the leather pouch would stretch and burst. By 1982, scholars had rediscovered the first-century wine-toting truth and were humble enough to throw the bottles out of the New King James Version and speak of the wineskins once more.

Best I can tell, our seventeenth-century brothers and sisters simply got tangled up in their modernity and made a bad translation call. Which sets me up to drive two things home: first, we can read the Bible wrongly, based on our lens. Second, the Bible can be trusted partly because it is not translated in a vacuum. There are many original manuscripts, and there has been a great deal of translation work done by those who want to remain meticulously loyal to the Word.

Given that our faith has a book, its authority has a profound effect on the faith itself. Simply put, if you don't trust the Bible when it talks about people walking on water, then faith will give you that sinking feeling.

It's a long and agitating road for the Christian who struggles to trust the Bible or tries to live the faith without it.

Think about how central it really is to the Christian experience.

Bible studies.

Bible sermons.

Bible community.

Bible verses used to defend ideas.

Bible verses used to attack ideas.

Bible quizzes, crafts, and debates.

Let's take one step further in. One matter that is often debated is whether the Bible is inspired or not. This is something different than finding the Bible inspiring. How involved was God in its writing?

Was the writing of the Bible **inspired** by God?

How much different might the Pentateuch sound if Aaron wrote it instead of his brother Moses? How much Moses do we hold in our hands? Did the Spirit of God dictate every single word, or did God give some creative license to old Moe? Was Moses one of the greatest storytellers of all time, or was he simply the man with the means to get it all down?

How about Paul?

Do you feel like there's a hint of Paul in Galatians? Before he transitions to speaking about love, joy, and peace, he offers 15 words that make middle-school boys giggle: "As for those agitators, I wish they would go the whole way and emasculate themselves!"[3]

Now, to be fair, this isn't a prescriptive text; it is describing Paul's thoughts, not encouraging us to attack. But, wow! I mean, perhaps he had Genesis 34 on the brain. You remember that time Jacob's sons revenge-murdered every male in the city because the golden boy in the palace raped their sister? Do you remember how they were able to overtake so many men on their home turf? They convinced every one of them to get circumcised, and then on the third day while they were still sore, they were sitting ducks.

So we ask, "If the Bible was inspired in its writing, *how* was it inspired in its writing?"

Were the ideas inspired?
Were the inspired words directly given to the human writers?
Or were the authors inspired?

3  Galatians 5:12, NIV

Paul, in his first letter to the church in the town of Corinth, makes a distinction between his words and the words of God. This creates some tension for those who are thinking more deeply about what they hold in their hands. *How inspired is this? What are the mechanics of how this is inspired?*

Andy Stanley preached the most memorable sermon that has ever *happened* to me. It was experienced, not only heard. He simply walked us through the life of Joseph and asked, "So what did Joseph do?" Then answered, "Joseph did what any one of us would do, if we were absolutely convinced that God was with us."

Any one of us would share a scathing dream with a ruler who could have us killed, if we were absolutely convinced that God was with us.

Any one of us would run from a sexual escapade with a high-ranking official who might be highly perturbed by our refusal and have us killed, if we were absolutely convinced that God was with us.

Any one of us has the wisdom to protect an entire nation from a predicted famine, if we were absolutely convinced that God was with us.

Any one of us would forgive those who attempted to murder us and sold us into slavery, if we were absolutely convinced that God was with us.

The sermon had humor.
It was profound, and clear as a bell.
It had a story with a theme. It was an experience, it caused me to wonder at God, it respected tradition, and seemed to meet me in a place that was relevant.

Here's my point.
Pastor Stanley is funny, profound, and clear.
He's a great storyteller who is experienced and fears the LORD.
Andy Stanley has a way of speaking to every person in the room in a way that is accessible.

It was a large conference, but God met me there.
The Holy Spirit planted something in me there.
Scripture came alive to me there.

Andy Stanley ministered to my soul there.

My point is that there seems to be a theme for Yahweh—He works through people.

He works to empty us of pride, but not of personality.
He is our strength, but He also uses our strengths.

Whether it's the kindness and generosity of Nick's soup on the porch or the fruits of the Spirit in Jillian's coaching of T-ball, God seems to be tenaciously partnering with humanity. My suspicion is that the scriptures are no exception.

Perhaps some of us have had a hard time trusting that the scriptures are inspired by God because we unintentionally thought that meant the same thing as being word-for-word dictated. If this is so, then any hint of the author's style or preference casts a shadow on the whole premise.

I'm convinced that the Bible I hold in my hand is inspired, much like soup when I'm sick, or an out-of-the-blue encouraging text on a Tuesday evening, or the homeless outreach a few blocks away.

Scripture oozes with the sense that God is jealously watching over it.

Sixty-six books that harmonize like they do?

Forty-something authors?

Written over 1,500 years, where sinister cooperation would be impossible?

Different languages, on different continents, under different circumstances?

Written through the rich and the poor, the educated and the uneducated, Jews and Gentiles?

In some settings, I've tried to make a habit of sharing godly wisdom without quoting the source. I call it *conversational plagiary*. I've simply removed "the Bible says" from my vocabulary and have watched the impact it has had without the added static of a religious text. I can trust it is inspired because I've witnessed the Truth setting people free.

The other day, I was shooting the breeze with an unbelieving friend who was fighting with his girlfriend. I said, "Well, you know, a gentle answer seems to defuse anger in a way that an angry answer doesn't." He had absolutely no clue Solomon wrote that in Proverbs 15. My friend's face fell. He kicked a bit of gravel and simply said, "Wow. Never thought of that."

Here's my point.

The scriptures are inspired.

They just hit different. They mature their readers. They convict, direct, comfort, and kinda sorta do a lot of the same things God does. It's almost like they introduce us to His majesty and His goodness, and we don't even need to have our background checked to get a meeting with Him.

**Inerrancy** is another major field of consideration as we contemplate putting that last Bible in the garage sale.

Inerrant: without errors.

Many have walked away from the Christian faith in part because they're convinced, or at least suspicious, that the Bible doesn't have its facts straight. It doesn't help when your faith has been built on an all-or-nothing, black-and-white, certainty-based treatment of the Bible. Some church traditions simply collapse without a perfectly logical, proven, square, plumb, and balanced Bible framework. For some, every stroke of the pen is a linchpin.

A linchpin is the small pin that passes through an axle to keep the wheel on your car. There's a community within the church whose Bibles rattle with linchpins. Linchpins everywhere. Spelling, grammar, dates, weights, numbers, stories, hours, and accounts. They all must add up in a way that they can all understand or they can't trust anything between the covers. After all, the Bible must show its credentials, like a lanyard or military patch.

Both literalists and liberals must guard their hearts against pride as they interact with the scriptures. Neither God nor the Bible feels threatened by our critique. We're just not that smart.

The ambiguity around how it all lines up might just be God's grace protecting us from truth that would crush us.

So, does the Bible have errors?

Earlier, I argued that we can't live by faith without faith. Let me add that we must read the Bible with faith as well. My friend Jason reminds me that my answers today will be better answers tomorrow, but I want to highlight some things as I understand them today.


Does God have feathers?
Does Yahweh ride on clouds?

How big are God's "hands" anyway?

If Earth was created in six literal 24-hour periods, then how did trees grow from seeds, mature, and produce more seeds on the third day? I've planted trees. It seems as though these Eden trees were on quite an accelerated track. On the other hand, if Earth is billions of years old, how was there a morning and an evening each day?

After some time of hearing both sides of this debate, it seems to me that we have an interpretive disagreement, not a contradiction of facts between science and the Bible. And that's just the thing that keeps me up at night; some have scrapped the Bible when I wish they would have just scrapped their all-or-nothing certainty.

I do not see errors in the Genesis text; I see a marvelous God who spoke to an ancient Hebrew and together with him wrote the most foundational book in all of human history. It's poetic at times, it's puzzling at times, it's profound at all times, and I wish I were a pro at finding its profundity.

When I considered how it was common practice to only list living family members in conversations, I didn't stress over the discrepancy between 1 Samuel and 1 Chronicles attributing seven or eight sons to Jesse. That does not add up to an error for me.

I had such a hard time with the idea that God creates some people only so He has someone to whack when this whole judgment day goes down. I mean, we've got the clay pots and fine china of Romans 9, and you'd better hope you're more like a gravy boat than a clay pigeon. That is, hope you're precious, not targeted.

Early on in my following Jesus, it was great to hear reasoned debates about sovereignty and just how conditional God's election may or may not be. These debates kept my mind engaged in the process of theology instead of causing me to check out due to a hard-line understanding of a deeply complex doctrine that impacts all humanity's eternity.

If you've heard that "everything happens for a reason," and that "God works in mysterious ways," and that "God is in control," then you might see your eternal destiny more like a game of Yahtzee than the finished work of Jesus. I learned some things about what God prescribes, what God permits, and what God chooses to do providentially. What once was a biblical error or difficulty about who's saved or not is now a Monet whose theme is God's mercy and restraint as He stays attentive to the state of fallen humanity.

An internet favorite is the problem of how many angels were at the tomb of Jesus. Was it one or two? Mark seems to say two, while Matthew seems to say one. Which was it? If we slow down, we realize that we caused an error by adding the word "only" to Matthew's account. Mark says they saw two, but Matthew says that one said something. It's light work to defang this biblical difficulty, but if you're already flooded by church frustration, sexual temptation, or pressure from your roommate, simple misunderstandings like these embolden you to sleep in on Sundays and find a source for truth and authority you can trust: *you*.

Perhaps you've noticed a certain bravado that seems to characterize those who are first to "defend the Bible." I hope this book in some way is a defense of the Bible, but I hope its volume and tone have conversational coffee breath.

I wish I could invite each and every person looking to break free of biblical literalism over to my house for a few hours. I'd go to bed early the night before, brew better coffee, and meet you at the door, and we'd kick our feet up on the coffee table. We'd belly laugh, listen to one another, and learn to get comfy in our own skin. I'd then encourage you to read poems like poems, eyewitness accounts like eyewitness accounts, histories like histories, prophecies like prophecies, and apocalyptic stories like apocalyptic stories. Together we'd learn to major in majors, minor in minors, and most of all, like siblings' weekend, we'd learn to live as sons and daughters of the Most High God.

We'd let ancient explanations be just that. We'd let letters be letters, and we'd let the scriptures do the work they set out to do, without acting like a Psychology 101 college student on Christmas break. You know that one time everyone winced as Tiffany went around the room, flawlessly solving every mental, emotional, and interpersonal issue present? Meanwhile, Uncle Shane popped an almond into his mouth and reminded us that Tiffany still can't drive a stick-shift. Maybe we approach scripture with a little humility.

I do not wish to misrepresent my inerrantist brothers and sisters. Being an inerrantist—one who believes there are no errors in the Bible—does not equate to being a literalist as outlined above. A great number of inerrantists believe the Bible contains no errors, and also know that some things are not to be read literally. They also admit that some things are descriptive instead of prescriptive, and demonstrate a great ability to read the Bible in a faithful and humble manner.

Let's take a moment to discuss a couple of contentious texts often referenced in the inerrancy discussion.

First, Leviticus 11 seems to give the idea that grasshoppers have four legs, when indeed Rabbi Google shows me that they have six.

Where do we go from here?

Unfortunately, the flippant ex-inerrantist might scrap the whole Bible because of a two-leg discrepancy. That's a weak linchpin.

For the fragile inerrantist, the question lingers. If Moses can't correctly count grasshopper legs, we're going to have to throw out the Ten Commandments—or maybe it was six or four rules for life.

We might commonly hear this sentiment in statements like, "If you can't trust it all, then you can't trust it at all."

Thankfully, there are thoughtful and even-keeled inerrantist responses to this text—there are those convinced the Bible has no flaws who might ask us to consider a bit more.

Modern specifications of species, genome, and family were yet to be honed at the time of this writing. Moses used characterizations like "kind" as opposed to our modern delineations like "phylum" and "class."

The Torah's groupings are logical, yet different than the ones we use today. For instance, the Bible's "flying things" groups insects and birds together. Today, we classify bats as the lone flying mammal and do not classify them as birds, but Leviticus 11 does. After a little consideration, how strongly does this 2,700-year-old classification erode your trust in the Bible? You can see the logic in classifying a bat as a bird, right? I hope a raven looks more like a bat than I do! But we're not putting that to a vote.

It seems reasonable to note that migrating grasshoppers like locusts have four legs for clinging, climbing, and crawling, while their rear two appendages, which look much different, are used for jumping. Again, Leviticus dives into how the rear "legs" are jointed differently than the other four "legs."

So, we might do well to ask ourselves, after giving it a little more thought, if it is more reasonable to chalk this up to a biblical error or to see evidence of an ever-sophisticating understanding of nature?

Before we move on, let's look at one more frequent refrain. It's common to hear Christians who do not hold to an inerrant view say things like, "The Bible is perfect in matters of faith, truth, and life."

In other words, "The Bible nails it on the important stuff, but it's only near perfect on the unimportant parts, like insects." They might say something like, the Bible is there to do theology, not science. This line of thinking makes a bit of sense to me.

For instance, they might say, "Don't discard the birth of Jesus in Matthew 1 simply because the genealogy of Matthew 1 doesn't add up at first glance."

While that makes sense, I still find it hard to confidently say that we humans are very good at discerning what's important and what's not.

It's easy for me to imagine, based on what's in vogue, that we might throw out some bedrock truth that at the time seemed insignificant.

I must confess that my importance radar has needed recalibrating over the years; I've simply gotten it wrong in the past. I must humbly also recognize that the closer the Bible gets to rebuking me, the more tempted I am to see what it says as an *unimportant* truth.

Perhaps you've buried your embarrassed head in biology class as someone "rejects" science because the Bible "contradicts" it.

There are definitely moments for this sort of science-class challenge in scholarly halls, but I suspect that some are unnecessary.

To be sure, this can be a crisis moment for many, but I've found that with some time, those who make peace with the cognitive dissonance and commit to making this a subject of study, tend to find reasonable harmony between scripture and scientific journals.

May we not be too quick to scrap our Bibles.
May we not be too quick to scrap geology.

May we hold them in tension.
And take a deep breath.

Genesis 1:7 is one such place for inerrancy campers to practice sitting in the tension between science and the Bible. This bit of scripture speaks of the waters below the air and the waters above the air.

For some, this is clearly a biblical error brought on by the writer's contemporary idea that the earth was surrounded by water, like a giant water balloon over the earth, and this has clearly been debunked.

For some, there was a great water layer, but it ruptured at the time of the worldwide flood.

Still others hold that this text is simply speaking of clouds.

I hope you're giving some real consideration to how some are able to hold two conflicting truths without feeling conflicted. They hold their Bible and their beaker in great harmony.

It's important to mention that most proponents of the inerrancy view often distinguish between original writings and copies. It's not rare to hear that the Bible is inerrant in its original writings, not inerrant in every copy or translation.

Whole books have been written to discuss Bible difficulties. You can buy one or two, and I'd recommend it, but we're moving on.

Scholars also speak of the Bible's claim of infallibility. This is something different than inerrancy. Simply put, the claim of infallibility invites the question "Does the Bible accomplish what it sets out to accomplish, or does it fall flat?"

The poetic metaphor in Isaiah 55 likens God's word (which includes but is not limited to the Bible) to rain. It doesn't return to its lofty position in a thundercloud without watering the soil and subsequently causing things to bud, blossom, and reproduce. Infallibility's claim contends that the scriptures have a way of never coming home empty-handed. They always bring home the bacon. Kosher bacon of course. Or turkey bacon, I suppose.

Is the Bible the *Little Engine that Could*? Does this collection of wisdom have a track record of winning? I would never want to give the appearance of liking Tom Brady, but is the Bible the Patriots of the Brady and Belichick era? Can the scriptures be trusted in matters of faith and living?

Whether we can articulate it or not, we're all asking this question: Does it work?

Are church folks healthy?
Do Christians build great societies?
Does God know what He's talking about?
When trusted and obeyed, does the Bible encourage and empower people to work for the good of others?

Let me illustrate this creatively. I'll use the anniversary poem I'm writing for my wife, Mandy.

Roses are red
Violets are blue
Sugar is sweet
And your lips are too

Imagine her getting tripped up by the fact that some roses are white. We had white roses at our wedding, so imagine if she fell into a rabbit hole around that. My wife is smart. We have a healthy friendship and an active romance. I'm sure she'd smile and lean in, and the kids would quickly break us up. My poem's infallibility is greatly influenced by the relationship between the author and the reader. My words are received with the precursor of relationship and understanding.

My poem could share truth through literature, without being literally true.

As I've waded through my Bible questions, misunderstandings, and perhaps irreconcilable difficulties, I've found it wise to trust the infallible nature of the scriptures because I've discovered a thing or two, I've turned a corner or two, and I've matured a time or two.

I still don't quite know what to make of Jesus' words in John 20:23. On one hand, He seems to be saying that the disciples can forgive people's sins, but on the other hand, He could be saying that He trusts their discernment. To be honest, I really don't know what to do with it.

Can we live by faith even while wrestling with our faith? Can we trust God's ability to get us where He wants us to go?

It's extremely humbling anytime someone shares a story of how my sermons have helped them. Preaching is like handing someone a magnifying glass. It might help them discover something remarkable, or they might start a fire in the leaves. I can tell you, my sermons have errors, they are fallible, they are imperfect, and sometimes they're inspired, but even with such a disadvantage, God has used them. God has used you. God has even found a way to use me. May we wade through our Bible trust issues like the guy in the book of Mark who said, "I do believe; help me overcome my unbelief!"

Let's imagine that I have a friend who exaggerates. Every song is either his favorite or the worst. He has been on his death bed six times. He has the best week at least once a month, and he's always meeting the funniest person he's ever met. The other day, he borrowed my truck and said he'd have it back by morning. I trusted him. He's a man of his word. He did. He replenished the gas he used, left it on country radio, and cleaned out the bed. After all, those are the rules. While I can't trust every word he says literally, I can trust him. His character is not in question just because he speaks with an exaggerated tone. I'd lose a friend if I somehow confused these two realities.

We trust people to the degree to which we know them, and to the degree to which they prove trustworthy.

I didn't fear him borrowing the truck, but I also didn't conclude that his new friend was actually funnier than me. Let's be real. I'm hilarious.

We doubt sources to the degree to which we find reasons to doubt them.

We trust sources to the degree to which we find reasons to trust them.

Against this backdrop, I find people quite harsh with the Bible. We have more grace with exaggerating friends than we do with the scriptures. If I can't figure out why Luke said Lysanias ruled Abilene in 27 CE, when we all know he ruled Chalcis about 50 years prior, then I can't trust the Proverbs, or accept Jesus' teachings, or grant that the Ten Commandments are profound and applicable to today?

Overreact much?

Spoiler alert: there were two rulers named Lysanias.

Luke was vindicated by archaeologists some 1,700 years later, but not without the babies and bathwater strewn about the lawn of forty generations.

The phrase "Consider the source" works much to Luke's favor. Sir William Ramsay of Oxford University is celebrated as one of history's greatest archaeologists. In an effort to dismiss the book of Acts, he dug into Luke's claims. He found fifty-four cities, thirty-two countries, and nine islands, just as Luke said. He concluded that Luke was one of the most accurate historians to date. Because of this, he came to believe in Jesus. Why? Because we trust sources to the degree to which we find reasons to trust them.

I humbly ask, are you using a sensible trust grid when it comes to trusting the scriptures?

Every night that I find myself reflecting on God's character, I find more reasons to trust because the more I know Him, the more trustworthy He proves to be.

Like, lots more.

Not all faith is blind faith.

It's a mixture.

I trust because I see some things, while trusting things I don't see. You need look no further than home or work to see this reality in play.

I trust my car to get me to work. I don't understand the adaptive cruise control, but I do know that it slows and speeds up the vehicle based on the speed of the car in front of me and has faithfully gotten me to work and back for seven years. I also see that the tires aren't flat, and that it's been locked all night.

It's an unfair simplification to pretend that all theology is blind faith.

If religious differences were merely "You blindly trust that, and I blindly trust this," then there'd be nothing left but preference.

But much faith is encouraged by sight.

The Bible is historical, it speaks geographically, there are eye-witnesses, it makes claims that can be tested archaeological-ly, and the validity of the scriptures can be assessed by reading books that were written at the same time about the same things. And lastly, if one is honest, they must sit with the Bible's prophet-ic accuracy.

If my eyes find reasons to trust, they lend courage to my feet to take the next step, even into the pitch black.

Many Bible problems are simply due to the fact that the level of biblical illiteracy is appalling. There seems to be so little Bible reading and even less study, with only a trickle of understanding and obedience.

There's still a guy somewhere feverishly tearing through his over-sized Bible, looking for that verse that says "God works in myste-rious ways." I told him I'd give him $100 and let him "preach the Word as it should be preached" if he found it. Spoiler alert: it's not in there. It seems to be true, but it's not found in the scriptures. It's hard to say this out loud, but some people just aren't very skilled at reading the Bible.

Let me illustrate.

It's a tragedy that I have no words of advice for Macbeth, other than to hold on for a few hundred years and head to Edinburgh for the festival. I've just lost some of you, and that's, in part, my point. There's a steep learning curve to reading Shakespeare, and while the Bible is remarkably accessible to all, it has its own learning curve. If we aren't willing to engage it with at least as much study and care as we would Shakespeare, we will read it poorly. I know from personal experience how to exegete the Bible poorly.

C. S. Lewis says something similar when he says, "If they cannot understand books written for grown-ups, they should not talk about them."[4]

I've lived the majority of my life in Christian community. Like the bald eagles down by the river, our church is not constricted by a denomination. We and our friends are nondenominational, *and proud of it*!

Ironically, we stick together as those who don't need to stick together.
We are defined by being undefinable.
Sure, we have our ethos, traditions, language, and style, but we're too advanced to be trapped by denominational constraints. We

4  C. S. Lewis, *Mere Christianity* (London, England: C. S. Lewis Signature Classic, William Collins, 2012), 137.

don't do catechism. It's too boring, too regimented, and too much like our parents. We have set ourselves free to be completely inept in defending Christian doctrines. My mocking tone is covering up my deep concern that the church doesn't know the Bible very well. LORD, forgive me for my role in this.

No wonder a first-year high school ethics teacher can threaten to empty the youth ministry with pretty weak logic.

There's another quite human Bible problem at work here.

Some simply disagree with what the Bible says.
Try it sometime. Start a topical Bible study on the subject of tithing, sexual sin, divorce, or racism.

Many Christians simply don't respect the Bible.
They don't need it.
Don't know it.
Don't agree with it.

For many, the scriptures simply hold no authoritative position in their lives. Can you feel the difference between "I'll go to the authorities" and "This doctor is the leading authority on your son's lymphoma"? One might make us think of force, while the other speaks of mastery. To say I don't agree with the arresting cop sounds different than saying I disagree with Dr. Sheri.

It sounds so foolish to admit that you disagree with an expert.

It sounds childish and embarrassing.

Stop and think of this as it relates to God and His book. After a prolonged time of dismissing God's authority, we find ourselves in a culture that's comfortable disagreeing with God to its own destruction.

LORD, I humbly admit that my defiance has led to ruin. I have been ignorant and stubborn. I have foolishly disagreed with Your expert shalom. LORD, You will not be mocked, at least not forever.

I saw a handsome pastor interviewed on a network talk show some years ago. The audience and hosts were celebrating and commending him on his courageous stand against racism. He stood up boldly on national television in the twenty-first century and said that racism is wrong, and I wholeheartedly agreed. When asked about abortion, he said that God's the judge, folks need to live out their own convictions, and these types of matters are between them and God.

Did you catch that?

He was commended for calling out something as a sin, then commended for not calling something out as a sin. "Great job making a judgment and speaking up" was followed by "Great job not judging and keeping quiet."

While I appreciate the nuanced nature of the issues at hand, I share this not to embarrass a fellow Christian or pastor, but to highlight the reality that it's easy to hold a standard that is both righteous and socially acceptable, while it requires great courage to maintain a righteous standard that'll get you canceled.

Are many Christians rejecting church because they fear God or because they fear the rejection of the many? My suspicion is that for some, it's super scary to disagree with culture, and not too scary to disagree with God.

The fear of man is still a thing.
It takes one to know one; I still struggle to fear God more than the crowd.

In all fairness, I must highlight that it's also scary to disagree with people in the church culture. So, the fear of man can hinder people from standing up against the church's cultural idols as well.

I'm often less like the lion of Judah, and more like the lion of Oz.

# 2 HOW TO AVOID THE COMMON PITFALLS OF MODERN DE-CONSTRUCTION

**My father was a mortician, so I've been around a lot of bodies who have given up the ghost.**

I've driven for funerals, helped transport bodies, and handled human brains in ziplocked bags. Autopsies are often required when the method of death has high stakes. How they died matters.

Murder or accident?
Grieving wife or life insurance fraud?
Choked on a hotdog or evidence of a genetic disorder?

I'd like to do a bit of an autopsy on those who walk through a season of spiritual remodeling. I'd like to explore how we do it wrong. Then, how we do it right.

# Pitfall 1: Move fast.

Sometimes I just need to vent. Sometimes I've just got to blow off some steam. I've been frustrated by our school system, people at church, worldwide pandemics, and car issues, but I'm mostly triggered by the political posts my friends make.

I've noticed a pattern: I'm always right; they're always idiots.

I can vent to my wife.
I can vent to my coworkers.
But I can't vent to Steve.
Nope, I won't do it.

Steve's the quietest listener, but inevitably he does that annoying thing where he slows me down. He isolates my statements. He clarifies their validity. And he doesn't let me off the hook.

Please, Steve, just reel me in and throw me back into the water. I don't want to be held responsible for my words, thoughts, actions, feelings, or questionable language!

But no. We wade through it as he seasons our conversation with the salt of over forty years of following Jesus. It's not pink and Himalayan, or from the sea, it's from the secret place of wisdom.

A couple of friends popping off about the latest headlines is one thing, but there are extreme consequences for rushing through deconstruction without investing the time necessary to slow down and take things one...thing...at...a...time.

It takes some real courage to take things one thing at a time, especially when things get tense.

It can sound a bit like this:

Me: "The church hurt me."
Steve: "Tell me how."

Me: "Well, it's really more about my upbringing. My parents were hypocrites."

Steve: "Now, what do you mean by hypocrites? I wonder if they were hypocrites or just imperfect?"

Me: "Well, the guy in my small group voted for you-know-who, and I just can't live with that."

Steve: "Were you able to ask him what went into that voting decision?"

Me: "Well, no, but isn't the church basically a factory for misogyny and putting women in their place?"

Steve: "Let's take some time to think through who leads at our church."

Me: "Well, my issue involves Bible interpretation."

Steve: "Which scripture?"

Me: "How dare you nitpick me!"

Inquiring minds inquire, and inquiring takes time.

As we navigate these spiritual waters, we need more soak than skim. My limited tubing experience tells me that speed makes one skim dangerously on top of the water. When someone brings a new boyfriend to the lake and I have a steering wheel, skim city! Like skipping rocks. Human rocks. Young block heads.

Joy unspeakable...for me

But in reality, skimming is dangerous.
It's also shallow.
It also requires speed.

We would all do well to slow down. Whether we know it or not, we are aching for a move of God to build strong, brave, seasoned church communities that are built on mentorship.

We need more Steves.

May God grace us to slow down and take things one at a time. May believers slow down when the person on the other end needs help wading through their flood zone of issues. Perhaps those in spiritual crises talk fast because the rest of us seem disinterested, busy, or annoyed.

I've invested hours a week, for years, systematically walking slowly through these waters with others. It's some of the most fruitful time I've ever invested. Now, I'll admit, pastoring provides time for drawn-out spiritual deep dives, so I can't expect the same schedule of everyone. But even while in a full-time ministry position, I know what it's like to fight for my schedule. It's a constant battle to tell the busy that I'm making time for these conversations.

The church needs to get much more comfortable strolling.
The church needs to whistle more.
We need to shuffle our feet, laugh, and simply make the time.
*Selah.*

Deep breaths, deep talks, and deep relationships.

Church relationships can be shallow.
Our church members should never look exasperated by the thought of walking systematically with someone who wants to take it one thing at a time.

And if you're a pastor, let's acknowledge that we can tend to make ourselves too busy for the things that make us feel insecure.

We lead almost every environment we're in. We're typically on our toes, and others are on their heels. There's nothing wrong with it unless we're avoiding risk and surprise to the point that we've insulated ourselves from being relevant.

"Relevant" is meeting a need.

So, if our door is locked and our schedule is blocked, it's highly probable that we're neglecting the needy.

People need their pastors.

That's part of being human. And if we need reminding, we're human. I know they're impressed with our building and following, and in a lot of ways, we've earned it, but we're going to need to prioritize slowing down. I won't quote some savvy business leader and tell you that if we want to speed up, we're going to need to slow down. Instead, I'm going to go old-school. Jesus modeled an unhurried pace, and did a better job than you or I have, even with our super user-friendly scheduling apps.

We're going to need to swallow our pride, book the appointments, and trust God to give us the words and ears of heaven.

Who knows? We might learn a thing or eight.

It would be dishonest to pretend that everyone who is deconstructing wants to take it slow all the time, but for those who do, the church should be prepared to stroll.

Interruption is a powerful weapon when arguing.

It's often much easier to change the subject than to change someone's mind.
It's easier than changing their attitude or perspective.
Perhaps we even interrupt ourselves if things are hitting too close to the toes.

———

Don't fall asleep around my father-in-law, Freddie, or you're headed for a face-plant. From fourth grade to now, he's been tying left laces to right laces. When you wake to score a cookie or use the restroom, it's two steps, then pain. It's incredible how two brisk steps can cinch those laces so tight you're going to need both canine teeth and flexible hamstrings to break the curse he's inflicted.

I've been meeting with a dear sister the past few months as we work together to undo her ecclesiastical knot.

We shared a moment a few sessions ago when she realized that her well-meaning Christian upbringing had greatly impacted her relationship with God. Hers was a house where any hint of sharing a personal struggle or discontent was seen as a selfish plea or ungratefulness, instead of a sign of maturity.

She learned to stay out of her parents' way, and she learned to stay out of Jesus' way too, mostly by hugging the walls and being sweet.

It was an incredible moment to see her realize that she was going to need to reject her family culture in order to dwell in the dwelling place.

There are times when embracing truth feels like leaving it, at first.

Perhaps Jesus is on the living room floor, inviting us to untangle the laces so He can walk with us in the cool of the day.

These are complex, Freddie-sized knots, and the environment needed for detangling is quite unforgiving, like a clove hitch in your tightrope, mid-stunt. For some, it takes much care not to hate your parents. It takes care to pray poolside in a bikini. You '90s kids know what I'm talking about. It takes care not to prefer to see a cooler in a clearing as *your church*. A pyramid of cans is no match for the sacred assembly. When it comes to church, the great theologian Alan Jackson humbly reminds us that sometimes we never know how much that muddy water means to us.

Sadly, too many of us grab the scissors and cut ties with church, faith, and mystery. I've far too often believed a great lie that if health, reconciliation, and truth are really worth restoring, they should come easy. If God wants me that bad, He should work for me.

So here we sit, like toddlers on the grocery aisle floor.

It's bumper to bumper on the road headed away from Christianity, with every car driven by those "doing the work."

Some are shocked to learn that oncoming traffic is "doing the work" as well, one knot at a time. They're working to connect with God and His people, especially when it's hard.

It's going to take work, and I'm proud of anyone willing to slow down, dig in, and get back up!

# Pitfall 2: Harmonize.

Jesus' followers were shocked to hear that the Prince of Peace came to make war. Thousands of years later, it's still upsetting for many modern followers. No swords or flags, but Jesus' commands are still a pill going down sideways. Deconstruction proves to be quite handy for those trying to eliminate all conflict between the Kingdom of God and the culture of the world.

Water and oil.
Light and dark.
Dogs and bigger dogs.

We're a long way from the pop-punk band MxPx from the PNW.

We're a long way from Third Day's heyday. I was in high school in the '90s. We did all we could to find Christian versions of secular bands. MxPx was Green Day for Christians, and Third Day scratched our Pearl Jam itch, minus the urge to shoot up in the alley.

Our parents had mistaken style for righteousness.
God's music had a narrow sound.
Our parents had mistaken style for unrighteousness.
"Drums are the devil's instrument."

They had confused style and virtue, and we were here to correct them.

The independent Christian underground scene that we were part of sought to make Christian music cool again. We screamed into microphones, ladies grew their armpit hair out, and we had CDs that weren't embarrassing.

Modern sounds with righteous messages.

It felt like we were taking a giant step forward, and we were!

Like so many spiritual renewals before us, the old message learned a new language, and grunge was our native tongue.

It's no wonder the church guy who lobbied so hard against us was still clutching his King James Version, saying, "If it was good enough for Paul, it's good enough for me." Which sounds great if it weren't for the fact that Paul had been dead over a thousand years when the King James was translated.

It serves as a classic example of loving the language more than the message. Wouldn't it be troubling to see the church aggravated every time the Tyndale people finished a new Bible translation?

We must love the message and welcome every language.

There's still some bad Christian music being made, but to some degree, our plan worked.

As an artist, I'm grateful for the sonic freedom I enjoy today. There's a lot less talk about which instruments satan enjoys and more actual art bursting out of redeemed and creative hearts. Creative folk, inspired by the Creator—it just seems right.

The emo rock scene has faded, but sadly, I'm much more emotional today about where this has landed us. Once again, we're caught in the tension of discerning between language and message.

Instead of merely adopting a cultural language, the church can be found adopting the cultural message as well.

At some point, we got comfortable with drums in church, and now we're comfortable with lies in church.

The church has enjoyed some years of being in the world, and it's quite comfy.

My atheist neighbor doesn't expect my girls to be sewing their own ankle-length dresses. They aren't shocked to see drums and hazers on the church social media. They aren't resisting Jesus because His people are colonial-chic. They don't expect archaic style. In fact, they don't expect much at all.

They don't expect healthy marriages.
They don't expect sobriety.
They don't expect wholesome talk.
They don't expect a different sexual ethic.
They don't expect joy, sacrifice, or nuance.

Once again, many Christians have mistaken style for message. There's a great difference between the two. Christ's message is simultaneously offensive and liberating. For some, being in the world but not of it is too cumbersome, so they let the world enter them.

I read somewhere that Nintendo's Wii was wildly successful due to the fact it met a need in a way no one expected.

Wii is where relevance and surprise collide.

We need more Wii in the church!
And we have Him.
His name is Jesus.

Jesus is the cornerstone.
Jesus is the capstone.
But Jesus is also the stumbling block.

Jesus is relevant in the most surprising of ways.

Jesus is our Wii.
Jesus is where relevance and surprise collide.
There is no cornerstone or capstone without stubbing your toe on

the stumbling block. The offense of the cross is the offense of chemo, is the offense of the Juneteenth riders, is the offense of a bomb disposal squad doing their job.

Jesus offends our pride, selfish autonomy, and lack of faith to bring life more abundantly.

So, here we sit as much deconstruction works to eliminate the aspects of the Christian faith that are embarrassing, in hopes of appeasing the world's ethic and God at the same time.

Call it love. Call it contextualization.

Call it loving your neighbor.

Call it relevance, but often, it's cowardice.

We're playing peacetime poker in a war-time bunker.

We're oblivious.

We're shortsighted.

We're tepid.

Perhaps believers feast on Babylon because many lack a robust understanding of *why* sin is evil. They have been told what is evil without understanding *why* it's evil.

My friend Sean reminds me often that God's standards are not arbitrary.
This isn't field day in elementary school. God's not setting out orange cones and challenges just to keep the kids busy till lunch.

This is science.

There's a law of gravity and a law of integrity.

There are thermal dynamics and family dynamics. Asbestos causes cancer and lust dehumanizes the soul. If we can somehow get back to the back-and-forth, dialogue-based, Socratic style of teaching theology, perhaps God's laws will be treated more like gravity than like police officers. Only a fool drops a bowling ball on his head because he thinks gravity is busy giving someone else a citation. "I fought the law, and the law won" might be even more true about gravity than the sheriff's office.

It seems to me that the culture around me is progressively normalizing sin more each year. Whether you agree with me or not, perhaps we can agree that as Christians mature, there should be a growing sense that the world and its values just aren't a fit.

Get used to it, Christian.

Get comfortable with it.

This is our normal, living contrary to the world's values.

Ask yourself, are all of your convictions celebrated by unbelievers?

When's the last time you took one on the chin for Jesus?

I mean, when's the last time you took a deep breath, whispered a prayer, and came out as an unbeliever to the church of pop culture?

Wearing your cross is a choice, but carrying your cross is a command.

The future church has come to terms with the fact that they drink from a different well, breathe different air, and often live at odds with the majority. Not for the sake of being odd, but for the sake of being God's.

The church of the future is going to have to see itself as counter-cultural, or it will live frustrated, defeated, and impotent.

Impotent.

Like, not potent.

Powerless. Of no help.

And yes, impotent as in unable to reproduce due to its inability to wake up, if you will.

The future church is losing big deals because they're climbing Jacob's ladder more than the corporate one. The future church knows that living blessed doesn't always mean they get the promotion. They know that it often means they have a deep sense of God's delight when they're fired for doing the right thing. The future church is orienting its life around the church calendar more than the election cycle. The future church is more focused on serving its neighbors than agreeing with them. The future church seeks to see where you're coming from but cares more about where you're going.

The future church is faithful to God in the kitchen and in the bedroom. They've exchanged selfishness for hospitality and chastity.

The future church's extra car is a loaner for those who are struggling, and her raises are making more room for generosity.

The future church is something else. It is something other. Buried in the layers of the Hebrew word for "holy" is the idea of "other." To be holy is to be something other, something else, something set apart, something sacred.

If the church ain't something else, then there's truly nothing to see here.

Listen, the city bus is full of those who are exhausting all their resources looking for truth and direction. They're coming up empty, and the church could be the last stop on their journey, if the church is confident enough to share the truth, no matter how it stings.

Truth in love.

___

My grandfather's hands were cracked leather. His handshake was strong and dry. His hands were confident with tools. Tools obeyed and begged for mercy. His hands were gentle with the brisket and skilled with embrace. Something in me just knew I'd never have that kind of hands. Maybe it was two World Wars, maybe it was the Great Depression, maybe it was growing up on a farm, but people his age were tougher than us.

My grandma had it all together too. Nothing rattled her. She created moments for all of us to enjoy, kept the family running, and played the piano with fire. I've spent some time thinking about the spiritual toughness of seventy years ago. At first glance, Christians were more sure, less deceived, and stronger in their convictions.

Another book is needed to really think this through, but for now, I simply wonder why my grandfather's generation seemed to leave the faith less.

Maybe there really were far fewer who were being deceived. Maybe the Bible teaching was better. Maybe we shouldn't have scrapped Sunday school. Maybe we preachers should get off Instagram and into grammar and cross-referencing.

Maybe sermons that dangled us over fire and brimstone led to more on-fire Christians. And while I would not agree with much of the theology of those sermons, I must repeat that the fear of the LORD is still a thing. Healthy fear. Maybe we've focused on the fact that God is loving while forgetting the fact that God is also holy. God is not either loving or holy; He is both.

That's what makes His grace and mercy so valuable.
That's what makes His wrath so reasonable.

God has a mark and is able to restore our relationship when we miss that mark.

My guess is that, even more than all of this, the reason my grandparents seemed to leave the faith less is because they lived in a much less hostile culture than we do.

Perhaps there wasn't much reason to leave the faith because the church was culturally enmeshed and accepted at large.

I want you to see that cultures have gag reflexes.

Cultures are defined by what they gag on.

A culture can gag on divorce.
A culture can gag on greed.
A culture can gag on atheism.
A culture can gag on laziness, pornography, crude language, abortion, or skipping church.

On the other hand.

A culture can gag on sexual restraint.

A culture can gag on the idea of absolute truth.

A culture can gag on feeling trapped in an unhappy marriage, working a job you hate, the idea of drug laws, or going to church.

A culture can gag on the nuclear family.

**A culture can gag on Jesus.**

To be fair, we've made some headway in the past century. We gag on racism more than interracial marriage. We gag on socially pressured church attendance, simply going to church because everyone at the office does. We gag on some dumb gender roles.

But my premise is that in a lot of ways, my grandparents could live as Christians in America with much less resistance from their world at large. Perhaps there were just as many unbelievers, but they were quietly in church, whereas today, it's culturally celebrated to not follow Jesus.

The tide has turned.

The reflex has reset.

I won't say I've experienced persecution; that feels like an over-reaction, but I have experienced the headwind getting stronger. On my low days, it sure feels like following Jesus is taking it out of me.

# Pitfall 3: Do it alone.

It feels a bit clunky to discourage people from critiquing their spiritual family without the input of their spiritual family. Similarly, it's odd to say, "While you're working to figure out what you truly believe about God, don't do it unless He's in the room."

I've found that my frustrations and grudges with others just don't hold up once I get into the room with them. It's easier to roll my eyes at them over the phone, through text, or when I'm daydreaming about how rotten they are. But the conversation elevates once we get into the same room together.

It's almost like they are their own best defense. Their redeeming qualities shine through. I get subtle nonverbal feedback, I get context, and they're able to correct and further explain. The conversation goes from one-dimensional to three-dimensional in a hurry.

If it's easy to forget the things you love about your family, then it seems reasonable to consider that the same holds true with your spiritual family. And not to exhaust this line of thinking, but I'm convinced the same dynamic is at play when we think about our relationship to God.

For all his faults, at least King David went to God with his grievances and doubts. I'd like to think that even if he'd had access to the dark side of Twitter, he would have continued to give God an earful and remain in the assembly of believers, even in his most insufferable moments.

It's good for me to be reminded that the church is a body, made up of many members. The biblical metaphor speaks of eyes and ears. Within most healthy local churches, God assembles those who are gifted to lead: some who encourage, some who excel in generosity. We've got scholars, artists, administrators, and prophets just to name a few. With this in mind, we must remember that not everyone at our church is capable of helping with all of our conundrums.

And that's just fine.

Ask your pastor for help finding someone to walk with you. But stay warm to the body at large. It's easy, when frustrated, to grow cold toward a great many people in the church.

It's easy to see them as simpleminded, fake, or unloving, but take courage, and stay put.

Perhaps the greatest miracle you'll see is God assembling a support system right where you are.

If you're listening, you'll hear the idea that *decolonization* is necessary for deconstruction to work. As is indicative of the movement at large, the definition of decolonization varies, but one potential undertone is the idea that you must be alone to be truly objective.

Is it truly possible to be alone and completely objective?

I'm an emphatic *no*.

Depending on the circumstances, sometimes we must travel across town or meet up with believers from a different church to work through some of our issues, but my encouragement remains. If, for some reason, you can't do some of this with your home church, then continue to worship, pray, eat, and laugh with your tribe, while using the side hustle as a way forward.

More often than not, this will only prepare you to develop the ministry back home for whoever needs what you needed in the future.

In my garage, I have a growing collection of tools. When I'm living my best life, they are organized by purpose. Mechanical tools. Woodworking tools. Tools for supply-side plumbing. Tools for waste-side plumbing. Electrical tools. Pool tools. Concrete tools. Yes, every tool can be a hammer, but aside from that, tools are predominantly job-specific.

Wrestling with your faith is a spiritual endeavor; it requires spiritual tools.

We are fools if we think we can use the tools of the culture to remodel our house of faith.

Isolated critical thinking won't do the trick. Rage, accusation, and agnostic therapy will leave you roofing with a floor sander.

Your scribbled list of unresolved doubts does not make your manner unworthy, so take communion with that notepad in your pocket. God has supercharged the sacraments to make it easy to experience His grace in this fallen world. So savor the wine while you ponder the exact mechanics of the atonement. Eat the bread as you pray for an apology from the lady who served it to you. Open your eyes to see those around you. See an imperfect people, consider their lists, and consider that they too are placing their faith in Jesus because they're hung up to some degree as well.

Take a chance. Sing at church. Find those lyrics about desperation, faith, and dependence, and hit that high harmony part. Let the kid next to you know that it's normal to wait for a good answer. It's okay to still trust even when you don't know how in the world this all fits together. Worship in spirit and in truth. Where's your spirit? Where's your fighting spirit?

There's a great tool-to-job mismatch when we leave the Christian community to sort out our misgivings about the Christian community. The best of circumstances gives us access to thinkers, feelers, doers, and seers. The church is an eclectic community of those who have never been there, those who are right where you are, and yes, those who have been where you've been.

Small-group pool parties have a way of bringing perspective when the bestseller can't, because this is a faith job that requires faith tools, like community.

I wonder if there's a scenario where the wayward sheep is not lost but is unconvinced that he needs a shepherd.

Yesterday's grass was stale.

I see a shortcut to the watering hole.

I can travel faster without the flock.

What's that two-legger know about sheep anyway?

We all need a shepherd. We need the Great Shepherd, and we need a pastor. Like a real one. Like a real-life, schedule-keeping, desk-owning, Bible-preaching, joke-telling, hospital-visiting shepherd.

Preaching and teaching seem to play a very important role in the life of faith. It's a common occurrence for those who start wrestling with their faith to quickly remove themselves from the direct effect of preaching and teaching. They just don't need it anymore. They can't trust preachers, or they're mainly showing up to find the holes and disagreeable snippets, or it's not deep enough, or it's too deep, or they like to listen to five other podcasts instead.

Scripture is stuffed with instances of God using human speeches to lead His people.

Moses spoke.

David spoke.

Jeremiah spoke.

Jesus spoke.

Peter spoke.

Stephen.

Paul.

False prophets.

Whoops, that last one got ya, didn't it?

Jesus incarnated about 2,000 years ago and became the purest collision of heaven and earth. All God. All man. The church is the collision of heaven and earth. Our bodies are the collision of breath and dirt.

Preaching is the collision of truth and application.

Preaching is the collision of experience and study.

Both the shepherd and the Great Shepherd will collide with you.

Preaching provides an opportunity for us to practice shutting up, and it's good for us to shut up sometimes. If we spend too much time thinking, *The only thing missing is my voice*, we cease to grow.

Interjection can be the defense mechanism that works to hinder my transformation.

Sometimes I talk too much.
Sometimes I prove my point too much.
Sometimes I challenge ideas too much.
Sometimes I want the microphone too much.

Interrupting can be like opening the oven as the cake is rising. It's pulling a steak out of the marinade too early. It's only worshiping in circles where I can share my thoughts, and never in rows where I sit and let the preacher do his thing.

It takes *humility* to sit there.
It takes *honor* to sit there.
It takes *faith* to sit there.

Wrestle, go to church, take notes, circle back around, reason, and have follow-up dialogue. But don't alienate yourself from the good work God does in your heart through your faithful shepherd's preaching.

Allow me to make it plain.

When making crucial decisions about your faith, it is dangerous to disregard the people of God, preaching, teaching, and shepherding.

One last outworking of doing this alone.

There's a cocky arrogance to atheism. In some sense, I can understand agnosticism. But atheism requires a *certainty* that there is no God, and that's a bit like Mario in a NASCAR race. Cartoon cars are simple, but when actual rubber meets actual road, Mario is out of his league.

I've often been puzzled by the reality that the bar across the street is filled with those who applaud both open-mindedness and atheism. That's incompatible. At least agnosticism has the tinge of humility. It has humanity and reality. Agnosticism at least holds the possibility that there is a God. What the atheist rules out is the possibility that God is at work.

Paul told the little church in Rome that Jesus died a reconciling death and that He did it for those who were yet sinners, still sinning, still blind to the great advantage of the cross.

Before they turned to Him, He turned to them.

Dear friend, God is working behind the scenes. The back curtain is waving; the Spirit is active backstage. Can you hear the shuffling between acts? One day Jesus will stand center stage with a trumpet, a horse, and a choir. But for now, take courage. God has not left the building.

So, I dare you to keep the mysterious possibility alive as you wait.

I dare you to entertain the possibility that if there is a God, He could possibly be at work and quietly involved in your life right now.

We should always remember that God is working behind the scenes. Because, as we live in the awareness that God is at work, we soften our tone and pause to listen more.

If we believe that God is at work behind the scenes, we might wait for hearts to soften and put down our mallets. When was the last time you resisted the urge to manipulate or bully, and instead trusted God with the results? Your critique is probably warranted, but is there space for God to work, or are you trying to do His work for Him?

I love walking hand in hand with my daughters, but during the formative years, our strides often don't sync up. It takes some real effort on my part to match their stride so that we don't clash like an oval rolling downhill. And as they grow, they learn to match my stride. The more I remember that God is truly at work behind the scenes, that He walks with me in my formative and short-strided years, the more I seek to walk in step with Him instead of just marching for Him.

If you're convinced that God is working behind the scenes, you might believe your enemy's story of transformation and not feel the need to grill them on all the particulars.

Knowing God is at work might also cause you to acknowledge that the enemy is at work as well. And if that's really true, you might be more open to the idea that you're deceived.

There's always something supernatural going on.

Always.


If it's indeed true that God is at work,
we should be more balanced and



unhurried.

# Pitfall 4: Live above scrutiny.

Scrutiny tends to have a negative connotation, but it shouldn't. It simply means to examine something more closely, to pause and critically observe. Deconstruction celebrates scrutiny—a commitment to look at things more closely.

To do this, sometimes we need a little space to breathe. Like forming a circle in gym class, sometimes we need everyone to be an arm's width apart. We need space to ask questions, get into the minutia, and find clarity. To be sure, sometimes we ask questions simply to stir up dust, but at our best, we try to eliminate the cloud of ambiguity and pat answers—to get down to the good stuff.

It's common to search for a space that is safe. A "safe space."

But it seems to me that in our safe spaces, we buck against people scrutinizing us. I think we're doing it wrong if we're demanding that others don't scrutinize our scrutiny.Occasionally, I'll challenge preachers through my social media page with insights I've picked up along the way. I recently posted about thoughts I have on sermon prep and was met with a spirited rebuttal.
The main gist was that Jesus simply communed with the Father, and "out of that" came the sermon.

"What makes you think Jesus didn't do sermon prep?" I asked. I wasn't looking for a fight; I was open to a conversation.

There was no reply.

I suspect that safe spaces have become walls we hide behind—they have become fortifications from which we attack an idea or person.

If I demand a safe space to ask tough questions, I must not bristle at your asking *me* tough questions. Have you noticed your internal dialog that seems to tell you when your idea is weak? Have you noticed your temptation to protect your weak ideas from scrutiny?

If my degree in teaching has served me at all, it has served me in that I am quite comfortable with the Socratic style of teaching. It's incredible to watch lightbulbs come on in real time. The Socratic method has a pulse of questions and answers, and this back-and-forth ultimately succeeds as the teacher can tell from the questions and answers of her students when they have indeed mastered the material. Cramming for the test won't work. Selecting "C" will not do. Cheat sheets are of no use. And ultimately, respectful conversations create the seedbed for the best ideas to rise above the rest.

Here's an emotional roller coaster I've ridden a lot. Someone will invite me to a complex conversation about a complex issue, and I will get excited! I'll get my supporting materials together, pray for wisdom, and settle in for an extended time of reasoning together. Here's where the bottom of my stomach drops out: they oversimplify the issue and give a wildly simplistic conclusion that shuts down all hope of scrutiny and nuance.

At first blush, I'd think complex issues have complex answers. I anticipate nuanced solutions to nuanced issues.

Nope.

I get manifestos instead of discourse.

God has no sexual ethic for us because "God loves everyone."
Does that feel a tad too simple?

Macro-evolution is a thing because "I just can't do a talking snake."
Does that feel oversimplified?

Don't blink at my divorce because "God just wants me to be happy."
Too simple?

I don't do church because "The Western church is corrupt."
Quite simple?

Do you see a pattern of easy answers?
Oversimplification.
Reductionism.

# Pitfall 5: Skepticism is your superpower.

We have five children and all of them went through the "why?" phase. Every command was rebutted with, "Why?"

The sky is blue.
"Why?"

Because blue light scatters more than any other color.
"Why?"

Because gases and particles cause light to scatter and blue light has shorter, smaller wave lengths.

"Why?"


Go to bed.



But let's face it, it's annoying and antagonistic when one sees their skepticism as a virtue and God-given talent instead of using it as a learning strategy. For some, "Why?" is the end, not the means to the end.

Imagine an archaeologist finding meaning in digging, without the desire to find anything. An excavation site is something different than a sandbox.

There's an allure in certain circles to being the smartest person in the room—the most critical, the hardest to please, the most well-read. But one can reach a point where they are simply being critical, and that's just dumb. It'd be like refusing to drive a car until you know where the brakes' ceramic was sourced or phoning the state department to verify the badge number of the officer in the patrol car behind you or demanding a certificate of watts from Walmart's customer service before buying new taillight bulbs.

The goal of Bible study is to know God better.

The goal of a devotional life is to do justly, love mercy, and walk humbly with God. All of Jesus' words should be heard through the lens of His priority to love God with all our heart, soul, mind, and strength, and to love our neighbor as ourself.

The church's sin, the antagonistic spirit of the day, and the absence of mentors all contribute to wounded souls and skeptical tones.

**I should be mindful not to just flex my skepticism.**

Of all the disciples, I think Thomas would have at least Googled "deconstruction" in the days after Jesus' death. Thomas might have been that kid who went to the missions organization, got disillusioned, and came back with a chip on one shoulder and a tattoo on the other. He just couldn't take anyone's word for it that Jesus was resurrected. He couldn't even take Jesus' word for it. So when he finally encountered the risen Christ, he needed to see the nail marks and put his finger in Jesus' side. Besides that just being kind of gross, Thomas doesn't seem to be terribly gifted in the area of faith.

But

Jesus patiently let Thomas look the car over.

Jesus presented the evidence, made Himself available, and then said,


"Stop doubting, and believe."


Jesus doesn't, at least publicly, celebrate Thomas's investigation as deeper or better than the others. Jesus doesn't seem to frame the others as pushovers or gullible. Jesus seems to be saying that Thomas's need for more evidence was due to his doubt. It's unclear to me whether his doubt was a lack of faith or a part of his faith, but this one thing is crystal clear: Jesus said,


"Stop doubting."


It's over.

It's expired.

The ship has sailed.

Stop doubting.

There must be moments when we just stop it. We stop doubting, and we believe.

Let's not forget that some of the other disciples doubted the accounts of the women, which only adds to the layers.

Have you ever observed kids coming off a roller coaster? They're emphatic. They're happy to announce that they were the most daring, or their car was fastest, or they shouted the loudest.

Emphatic.

Weekly, I encounter what I call *emphatic cynicism.*

Like kids leaving the coaster, we can all be quite proud and childish about our ability to out-doubt the others.

"Well, I read a different study that said..."
"I mean, I hear what you're saying, but how can we trust that..."
You get the point.

When doubt becomes your virtue, you'll stand up tall, like a big boy or girl, only to find that your feet are in quicksand. There's a euphoria to the "prove it to me" attitude, as though doubt is the crowning mark of maturity—a moral apex.

But unfortunately, the adrenaline of ivory-tower doubt blinds you to the fact that you're actually in quite a dangerous situation. You're trusting something that wants to eat you.

**Much spiritual aggravation is built on a cultural assumption that there is no such thing as certainty.**

Ravenous doubt is cannibalistic, like gossip in the teachers' lounge. You know what happens the minute you leave the room? They roast you.

Doubt erodes the doubter, and before too long, nothing is sacred, nothing is mysterious, and nothing is beautiful. We get into the habit of taking cheap shots at everything, awkwardly laughing at funerals and in moments of human vulnerability.

Trust me on this: I squandered my preteen years with this sort of emphatic cynicism.

No one can satisfy the antagonistic.

The cynic is never impressed.

I once had a young man tell me that Taylor Swift was nothing special. At the time, she had racked up at least five Grammys and sold 50 million albums (she'd go on to do that multiple times). My friend expressed serious doubts about just how much secret sauce was in her mix. Her chord progressions were nothing special to him. The untrained singer sang elementary melodies, not to mention the formulaic way she bashed all of her ex-boyfriends.

Nothing special?

Nothing?

At what point does the house band consider that maybe there is something special going on with T Swift?

Maybe my friend simply mistook musical preference for unquestionable musical value. But I think we can all sense an unspoken undertone of naivety, or jealousy.

My friend has a great deal of musical knowledge, but that knowledge was blinding him from the very real power of simple chords, catchy melodies, and clever lyrics that feel true for millions of people. He couldn't see that good production, personal grit, regular exercise, and saying no to meth have led to Taylor Swift being a household name.

I'll leave it to my friend Sean to write the book on reductionism, but in a world that celebrates the uncertain, we get good at doubt, and we tend to devolve into reductionists quite quickly.

# Pitfall 6: Ignore the reality.

There are countless reasons for deconstructing, but some people just don't want to follow Jesus. They don't want to live as Christians. That's the truth as simply as I know how to say it.

I'm afraid deconstructionist language can be used to mask what is often the truth of the matter, even from those who utter it.

Could it be that sometimes we say, "The Western church is corrupt," or "I just can't do the patriarchy," or "I need some space," when the truth is that we simply don't want to live within the teachings of the Way?

So just say it.

Some don't want to follow Jesus.


Some don't want to live by faith.

Some don't want to humble themselves.

Some don't want to delay gratification.


When my friend Jason talks about this, he says, "If that's the case, just say it. Otherwise, it's self-deception."


**Shoot yourself straight. This pitfall helps you ignore the reality that you just want to live your life ignoring God.**


I'm deeply convinced that there's a growing hunger in God's people to live lives of radical freedom—a freedom and quality of life that causes a dry world to pant for Jesus' lordship.


I pray for every angsty heart to return to the reality that God is God. This is His good world, and He's inviting you into *shalom*.


Peace.

Peace with God, and peace with others, for all eternity.

Starting now.

# Pitfall 7: Reject all religion.

I've heard it said that God is about relationship, not religion. The only problem is that I can't help but notice that Jesus was religious.

Jesus was a Jewish rabbi.
Jesus taught in the synagogues.
Jesus studied at the temple.
Jesus celebrated the religious feasts.
Jesus prayed, taught, and built His teachings from concepts that He had learned through religious means.

Jesus was not against all religion; Jesus fought dead and hypocritical religion.

We need religion.

Religion is meant to train our schedules and souls to facilitate relationship with God and with one another.

I've got a friend who is battling addiction and is in recovery right now. He was telling me his story and I laughed at how, after three-day binges, he'd dial up something positive and encouraging on his radio. Christian radio would facilitate the grace of God in his life.

This might be the most controversial thing found in this book: God is using Christian radio to reach the lost!

I've encouraged individuals to continue to read a Bible they don't trust because religion matters.

I've encouraged praying to an unknown God because religion matters.

I've encouraged going through the motions at church because religion matters.

Religion creates an opportunity for surprise.

When it's dry and quiet, when it's confusing and there are unanswered questions, spiritual rhythms can expose you to all the beauty around you.

I remember telling the story of the prodigal son to a non-Christian who was hungry for spiritual rhythms. It was the first time he'd ever heard it. He mulled it over, and it was a beautiful surprise.

He wept.

Spiritual rhythms set you up to be surprised by the power of God's love and purpose, especially when you don't feel connected to God's love and purpose, and you don't want to practice the practices.

Much of the deconstructionist rhetoric frames all religion as empty, but one should stay committed to spiritual rhythms even when they feel trite.

I reluctantly wound up at Lakewood Church for a Saturday night service. When Joel Osteen took the stage and preached the exact thing the LORD had spoken to my daughter, London, and me a few hours prior, I was blown away. The power and might of God were on full display. But we only witnessed it because I religiously sur-rendered my skeptical heart to spiritual rhythms.

Many times, religious duties wear us out.
This might be by design.
I'll elaborate.

I dozed off for a while during the single greatest prayer meeting I've ever been a part of. As a youth pastor, I was camping with a bus full of teenagers.

Did I mention we were camping?

Listen closely.

Youth ministry camping and lock-ins are satan's playbook.

Let's get filth, hormones, poor sleep, lack of privacy, fire, and only zipper-tight doors in bed with highly emotional services, smoke machines, and oh yeah, dim lights—for effect.

Add to that, medical emergencies—and we had multiple.

One kid had a diabetic seizure in the middle of the night. One girl ate a pinecone and had an allergic reaction. To this day, we don't know if it was the pinecone or the animal urine that coated the pinecone, but my money is on the urine. Another young lady fainted at the chorus of "Shout to the LORD." It was a heat stroke, and a "head meets concrete" fiasco.

I was tired.
But that night, we prayed anyway.
It's that whole rhythms thing I was talking about.

We divided the room down the middle with duct tape. Girls on one side, boys on the other. In a rare and risky move, I encouraged the teenagers to bring pillows and gave them license to sleep if they needed it.

One of our students grabbed the mic and began to speak of God's fathering heart. She spoke the word "Abba" and God's Spirit came in a way I still haven't recovered from. Kids were confessing sin. New songs were sung. Not one eye was dry. There was weeping, joy, and prayer. Other languages were spoken.

When I am weak, God's power rests on me.
Even I'm surprised to be writing this ode to religious duty.

If we'll show up, in our less-than-ideal shape, God might bring revelation, or answers, or healing, or power, or beauty.

Keep showing up.

———

My first guitar teacher was Pastor Chuck, and I was wrestling a nylon-stringed classical guitar. It played like a baseball bat. My son, Hagen, is much better set up than I was. Hagen has a Stratocaster, YouTube tutorials, and a fairly able dad to teach him. He is getting to be a good guitar player.

If you want to master an instrument, do what we have done: hide the case, buy a stand, and leave it out all the time. No joke. Leave it on a stand in the living room, or if your roommates will let you, leave a guitar in every room. We are creatures of convenience.

Hagen never puts his guitar up. He never puts his guitar down either.

Excellent chefs practically sleep on the kitchen floor.
Good athletes live at the gym.

Skilled writers always have a notebook handy.

Yes, we form habits, but habits form us.

This is why we do well to stay committed to spiritual rhythms, even when they feel trite.

Keep praying, keep journaling, go to Bible study, and stream that worship album.

Keep being religious.

Not dead religious.

Alive religious!

# 3 WHAT WE CAN LEARN FROM THE DE- CONSTRUCTION MOVEMENT

**If we are humble, we might remember that the deconstructionist is made in the image and likeness of God.**

Then we might listen humbly and recognize that they make some valid points. Here are a handful, and what we can learn from them.

Let's listen humbly.

# Death to know-it-all-ism

There's a story I once heard about a lizard expert, a wonderful lady, a leading authority on all things lizard, and her appearance on a talk show. I've researched but can't trace its roots. Therefore, I tell it from memory and can't promise it's true, but it's true.

It goes like this. She was on a talk show...

To be helpful, I've always pictured her in a muted green jumpsuit with a plastic rimmed hat. The hat is brown with some sort of hard-hat qualities just in case her research is under a coconut tree or near a gorilla—because that's where I imagine the lizards hang out.

Anyway, she's on the talk show and for some reason, the host flippantly says, "You know everything about lizards, don't you?"
To which she quickly, forcibly, and almost disgustedly replies, "No, I only know everything I know about lizards."

Let's give her the benefit of the doubt that no one, the world over, knows more than she does about lizards. It still stands true that she only knows everything that she knows about lizards. Thus, it could also be true that there's always more to know about lizards.

Have you ever noticed that the more you know about something, the more convinced you are of the fact that there is so much more you can learn?
Her disgust came from her deep appreciation for the reptiles—almost a reverence—and the fact that lizards are so incredibly complex, beautiful, and varied, that it would be disrespectful for anyone to claim complete mastery.

I would like to elevate Yahweh to the position of lizard.

Please hear what I'm saying.

This lady held more awe for these reptiles than we hold for God at times.

The Trinity is a great help in my understanding the nature of God, but I have no idea what a conversation between the three of them sounds like, because I don't know it all.

The cross did something great; I just don't quite understand all that it did, or how it did it, or why it was necessary.

Substitute?

Victor?

Healer?

A bit of everything, like a kaleidoscope?

The spirit was hovering over something formless and empty, but there was something there—please explain. That something was chaotic and a waste, but there was something there.

My in-laws knew of a lady who drove her car on an empty tank for an entire summer. She believed God filled her gas tank—please explain. Yet, God didn't keep my car from blowing up someplace in Colorado—please explain.

Jesus condemned empty Sabbath laws but didn't speak (as best we can tell) directly about slavery. I hardly know anything about lizards, and I clearly don't know all there is to be known about God.

Many are turned off by Christians who know everything about everything.

I should remember that my knowledge about God will always be incomplete, and perhaps that's exactly what those in the throes of deconstruction have been trying to say all along.

# Jesus à la carte

Jesus discipled a guy named John, and he wrote a book that now lives in the New Testament. And yes, it's living and active there.

John tells a story, in the third chapter, of a time when Jesus was approached by a high-ranking religious leader named Nicodemus. Nicodemus was secretly inquiring about Jesus' credentials. It was puzzling for Nicodemus that Jesus knew the material, but they'd never had a class together. Jesus was impressively built, but had never been seen at the gym.

Jesus' teachings were powerful, learned, and disruptive, but He wasn't familiar or beholden to the establishment. And that can be agitating to the establishment.

It seems to me that Nicodemus never gets to the heart of why he's come to Jesus because Jesus seems to derail the conversation, as He does. Jesus brings the conversation to a grinding halt and poetically tells Nicodemus, and seemingly everyone else, that you can't even see the deeper realities around you if you don't begin with "Jesus is LORD."

Begin?

Begin with "Jesus is LORD"?

This can be a jarring idea—that faith in Jesus is the starting line of the Christian faith, not the finish line of the Christian faith.

I must confess, I've seen Christianity exactly backwards.

Do this.

Say that.

Go here.

In my mind, these things were done in hopes that we would be convinced that Jesus is LORD somewhere down the road.

But this is out of order.

We must *first* humble ourselves before King Jesus.

Enroll in Professor Jesus' classes.

Grab the life preserver and slump into the arms of lifeguard Jesus.

Complete surrender.

In surrender, the things we do are done because Jesus told us to. The things we say are shaped by the conviction that Jesus is the expert.

Full stop.

We move from here to there because we're chasing the footsteps in the sand. Don't worry about the patches where there are no tracks; your grandma will be happy to explain it to you later.

But seriously, call your granny every now and then.

For many, deconstruction seems like the most sensible way back to Jesus, because it feels like He got lost along the way in all the hustle. May this valid critique energize a return to simple, passionate, start-with-Jesus, Jesus following!

I am Jesus' humble disciple.
That should always be my starting position.
Nothing makes sense without that initial commitment.

Do you see that living like a Christian is not the same thing as living *as* a Christian? So, rest assured that you're doing this right when Jesus is your way and your source of truth, and your life is sustained under His capable care.

Dear friend, abide in Jesus, especially when the weather is great.

# Diversity Is Not a Four-Letter Word.

The most horrifying day of college for me was my first speech in public speaking class. I was panic-attacking before panic-attacking was something I'd heard of. Sweat pouring from every pore, nausea, and ringing in the ears. I hated it, but I got good grades, and the feedback was positive. I couldn't tell how much of it was legitimate or how much was sheer pity for the pasty kid who demanded to go last.

I managed to weave my way through most of college without any more public speaking. Then came my final year. It was a class focused on preparing us new teachers for the many different cultures we'd encounter in our classrooms once we landed the big-league jobs in elementary education. The class was set up more like a debate. Two tables, hot button issues, and away we went.

I found my niche.
Public speaking made me nervous, but public debate made me smile.

My strategy was quite simple: know my position, but really know their position. I also developed a habit of framing my opponent's position in the best light so as to get them to agree with how I defined their position. Then I addressed their character; I didn't attack. Just the opposite: I sainted them. This led to less of a debate and, instead, a knowledgeable and helpful conversation. My teacher ended up taking notice and forcing me to speak to 400 of the university's donors on behalf of the Education Department.

Yeah, public speaking was my prize. God's kind of sneaky like that.

Here's what I'm getting at: when the stakes are high, it makes a lot of sense to know the issue inside and out, from both sides.

C. S. Lewis said, "It is a good rule after reading a new book, never to allow yourself another new one till you have read an old one in between."[5]

**Deconstruction encourages variety and exploration. God's people should too.**

We should try to read young thoughts and old thoughts. We should expose ourselves to thinkers from cultures and races not our own. We should read the liberals and the conservatives, the mainline and the nondenominational, winners and those who didn't win.

The goal of living more widely isn't to reduce or dilute your convictions; the goal is to gain godly wisdom wherever it can be found.

I had a time in college when I tried to live on the other side of the abortion debate. I gave it an honest effort for about three years. While I couldn't maintain the position, my attempt to understand and believe forced me to grow, in both directions. I became more convinced and more compassionate.

5  C. S. Lewis, *Joyful Christian* (New York, NY: Simon & Schuster, 1996), 103.

# When the Ketchup Grabs You

I love burgers.

The smaller the joint, the better. The fewer the options, the better. My family has coined such gems as "Dirty burger places." The burgers are clean but the ductwork is not. My wife's quality control seeks to determine just how sticky the bottled condiments are. Inevitably, the most delicious of spots have self-adhesive ketchup bottles.

Accumulated grime.

Seasoning.

"Character," I say.

Mandy smiles and prays.


Some walk into the church and want to run as soon as the waitress turns her back, because the church is in desperate need of some deep cleaning. Even unbelievers know it's a darn shame that the church is filled with hypocrisy, apathy, and bravado.

Somedays, it's painfully glaring how far we are from God's vision.


He desires *shalom*.

Peace with God, peace with others.

Heaven longs for an ecosystem of health and joy.


*Shalom* is a dad running from his work truck to meet his wife and toddler at the swing set. *Shalom* is an architect walking a tour group through his new house nestled on a rocky coastline. *Shalom* is a text message that clearly tells a friend that they're appreciated and inspiring to those around them.

*Shalom* is a church foyer filled with good coffee and laughter.

*Shalom* is bread, meat, and drinks that knit the extended family together.

This *shalom* requires purity.

Even through all the missteps, I'm grateful that the deconstruction-ist conversations have led to God purifying His church, even when it seems like an embarrassing scandal or a shake-up.

After all, the best day is the day of diagnosis. It feels like the worst day, but the worst day is actually the day before the cancer is found.

The Christian is directed in books like 1 Thessalonians to encourage others. They are encouraged to respect and admonish leaders. They are invited to love, live at peace, urge, and warn. The church is to be a place of patience, devoid of vengeance and back-biting. Christians must gather to pray, share joy, and fan the fire of the Spirit. Community is a place of prophecy and testing. We're asked to hold on to the good and resist evil. God uses this sort of environment to purify His people even more deeply—so deeply that their very souls ache for the day of His return.

I see recovery, apologies, new songs, financial generosity, and the old and young connecting deeply.

When we close our eyes and engage a hopeful imagination, we actually believe this is possible. But too often, we open our eyes to find a decaying church. That said, some are so inspired by the prophetic picture of life, health, and *shalom*, that they begin to work toward it, no matter what they see in front of them.

Many of you who are reading this desire a pure church.
I'm inspired by you, and I'm proud of you.

We need your prophetic imagination.

Purity might demand that we detangle scripture. Like a boat prop in the weeds, God's words can get bound up. Scriptures can be used out of context. Stories can be used to prove the wrong point. Sometimes we miss the point that was obvious to the original audience, simply because we are not the original audience.

Some nights, when I'm brave, I sit with a chunk of scripture and let it read me.

No varnish on the page, no dancing around its sharp edges.

Just me and the words. It's cold water to a sunburned spirit. It's a chisel on my blocky heart. My ego is its target. No slick conference speaker is there to soften its blow. No restroom breaks allow me to avoid answering the question. Yes, sometimes I seek a detangled *shalom*.

The nun who pulls back the curtain.
The accountant who starts a sexual addiction recovery group.
The pastor who seeks out therapy.
This is the road of purity.

----

Christian post-high school internships can offer an incredible opportunity for students who have not taken on the weight of family and career just yet. It's also a classic "get the fruit into the Jell-O before it sets" moment. These programs are intense. They can be extremely focused, and often impact the flight path of many lives.

They have also wounded many.

When you elevate and glorify youth, you'd better be prepared to deal with the disorder that comes with inexperience, arrogance, and baptismal hot tub parties, with bikinis and speedos. Yes, that happened.

There's a delicate balance to managing free labor. Without clear expectations up front, it's easy to work a volunteer eighty hours per week while they're raising their own support and assure them it's a *privilege* to be there.

Christian leaders would do well to pay close attention. Young leaders can get drunk on power; after all, they've been there three times longer than anyone else. Three years.

Too much responsibility.
Too little direction.
Too many hormones.
Too much abuse.

Some seek the purity and *shalom* of joyful employment in the church, and some get stitches for it.

# But, why?

My friend asked me to share the foundational truths that have led to my understanding of God's sexual ethic as he wrestled with how he was to specifically live as a Christian. It took me over a year to articulate them.

It was a labor of presenting why I believe what I believe. We spent roughly one hundred hours one-on-one. Yes, we grew as friends, ate good food, and sometimes just shot the breeze, but my friend asked me to slowly unpack the basis for my sexual convictions, and I can be long-winded. He grew up in the church and could recite what he'd heard, but then he read widely, thought deeply, and wrestled quietly.

We talked about marriage. I shared what I think marriage means for couples, what it means for kids, how it shapes families, and how families impact society.

We wrestled with God's ideal and legal unions.

We spoke of incest, orgies, and divorce. We waded through the major types of laws found in the Bible. We talked about progressive revelation, repentance, and life in this broken world.

We spent some time deciphering between temptation and sin. We had to talk about politics and law. We regularly stopped to look at the scriptures that shaped our sexual convictions.

We talked about identity, bigotry, and that one tree.

We talked about grace, truth, and the need for cultures to domesticate males. We talked about how women and children often pay the price for sexual sin. We identified unbiased research and threw some of the biased stuff out. I got angry. He was godly. We left some weeks unresolved. We cried. We prayed. We hugged. We disagreed on some things, but we landed at peace.

We did it right because foundations matter. Just like physical ones, there's a lot of mud and heavy lifting on basement day. But when it's built right, the framers, roofers, and trim carpenters all benefit from a job well done.

The *why* matters.

I must admit that my friends who have walked through a deconstructing season have stirred up a hunger for the church to know *why* we believe what we think we believe.

Maybe catechism wasn't such a bad idea after all.

# 4 SOME CULTURAL FOOTINGS OF MODERN CHRISTIAN DE-CONSTRUCTION

**Christian deconstruction didn't come out of nowhere like a Midwest microburst.**

It came from somewhere. That somewhere leads us to an Algerian-French philosopher.

In response to power-driven, narrow-minded academia, Jacques Derrida began to toy with boiling words down into an unintelligible soup, and then coined the boil "deconstruction." This is no single-origin meal, there are a number of other cultural values that have helped set the stage for today's movement.

In this section, I'd like to speak specifically about how the culture outside the church has laid the groundwork for much of this. But I hope we see, throughout this book, how the church's internal struggles have played a part as well.

In high school, I predominantly saw people as those who had values and those who did not. Those with values shared my values. And those who did not share my values did not have any, I figured. I've since come to realize that my greatest opponents live according to their values.

You can be stiff-necked and still have a backbone.

Whole cultures have values as well.

Cultures reinforce certain values in many ways through things like awards, commerce, and stories. For instance, our culture values rags to riches. We value acceptance, struggle, wanderlust, and a gluten-free diet. So let's look at the cultural values that have gotten us here.

# Movers and Shakers

Culture seems to be obsessed with shaking things up.

We celebrate disruptive businesses, loudmouths, and people who just say it like it is. And some of the most profound shake-ups happen when a culture's values shift. Once a new thing becomes normal, everything shakes.

Basements wiggle and rooftops crack.

The Hebrew prophet Haggai had a heart for the covenant people as they were returning from political exile. They had been mass-kidnapped by the Babylonians but were now being allowed to go back to Jerusalem to rebuild their temple. Some work had been done, but the people of God were just tired. They were lethargic. They were sleepy. But Haggai worked to stir them.

Shaking is a common tactic for waking both people and institutions.

In the second chapter of Haggai, the prophet reminds the people that Yahweh has a plan both for the temple and for them! He promises to make the temple greater than any previous version; the LORD promised to fill the house with His weightiness, and He would use this to shake the nations, the earth, the sea, and the heavens.

There's a whole lotta shakin' goin' on.

Nations are not static; they can be shaken.
Institutions are not rock solid; they too can be shaken.
Teams, cities, and families can be shaken.

One might be blind as a mole and still feel that we live in shaky times. It seems that every institution has been shaken.

I saw a skateboarding documentary shot at the height of the COVID-19 pandemic, as deserted Los Angeles highways became playgrounds for longboards, a beautiful reminder that cities, economies, and day-to-day routines were shaken.

Schools have been shaken. From low college enrollment to virtual learning to school shootings, education is shaking.

Riots and the sight of police fleeing their headquarters under threat of violence echo the shaking around law enforcement and civil order.

Today's typical family was once referred to as a "broken family." In a growing number of neighborhoods, a nuclear family is rare. And for some, the nuclear family is as threatening as the bomb bearing its same name.

Maybe it's just me, but media feels raw and shaken.
Modern lyrics leave so little to the imagination. So little.
If one were to try to push the envelope in a provocative way, where would they push?
It seems we've nowhere left to push.

Decorum has been shaken.

With streaming, the record industry sells far fewer actual records. Explain that to the record store owner in 1974. We don't even have to mention the black eye Netflix delivered to realize that media has been shaken.

Politics are toxic, violent, and near comical.
The capitol has been violently breached; Supreme Court justices have been hunted. Politics have been shaken.

The world of business has been reimagined in unprecedented ways. Bitcoin and online stores demand change.

Due to the pandemic, my local Dunkin' Donuts hasn't opened their dining room in years.

Cancel culture and the ease of consumer organization has created watchlists and reputation-crushing review apps that even the savviest of business owners can't overcome. A couple of years ago, a regional breakfast restaurant opened across the street from our church. Somehow the owner's political views were used online to encourage vandalism and ultimately run them out of town. The sentiment seemed to be, "We can't share a table if we don't share political views, even if the omelet is double-cheesed."

The business landscape has been shaken.

Spiritual deconstruction serves as a predictable outworking of a world that is comfortable with, if not lusting for, shaking.

Our cultural moment says that shaking is normal.
Shaking is admirable.
Shaking is necessary, and it's necessary

every second

of every one of your

waking hours.

There are times when shaking doesn't seem extreme enough.

**Culture seems to say institutions can't be trusted at all and need to be eliminated.**

If I threw a rock from our church's second story, chances are I'd hit someone who believes that life would be better with no institutions. "Can't we all just get along?"

"Resist the man."

Too many of my friends pride themselves on how long they've lived without eating McDonald's. The Foo Fighters are sell-outs, and community policing is the answer. Fake blood is poured on developers, and they are called bloodsucking capitalists at our city council meetings, but we can't seem to understand why we have so many potholes, and why parking fees are increasing.

When shaking is commonplace, some bring that approach to church, because, why not?

# You're Good

My social media is smeared with five basic assumptions, producing thousands of iterations.

"You do you!"
"Use your voice."
"Believe in yourself."
"You don't need to change; you're enough."
"Do the work."

I know, on the surface, it's empowering to celebrate individual creativity, strength, confidence, self-grace, and some level of courage, but often, these slogans irresponsibly feed the pride that says, "I'm always right!"

Go ahead and read through them again.
Can you hear the chant?
"You're always right! You're always right! You're always right!"

**Culture can convince you that you're always right.**

I did my time working in customer service, and I can tell you from experience that the customer is not always right.

It's quite dangerous to "do you" when you want to road rage. The world would be a better place if bullies quit using their voices. Many tears have been shed in *American Idol* auditions because people believed in themselves without knowing themselves. And Simon had a way of introducing people to themselves when they couldn't sing.

Gloriously awkward!

Loving ourselves "just the way we are" can often lead to an unhealthy maturity stall.

And "doing the work" is only helpful if the work helps us to become more like Jesus.

All this is to say that self-expression is not inherently virtuous.

Now, imagine with me a church board meeting full of people who are unquestioningly encouraged to say what they think. Now, imagine a college dorm full of students who have the same approach. And last, imagine those walking through a season of doubt with this baseline.

I'm grateful that some with pure motives have found the courage to speak up and speak out because sometimes we just need permission, but I think we can agree that sometimes we're wrong and we need to hold our tongues.

I want to speak to a particular outworking of always feeling right.

I too have foolishly trusted my *feeling right*.

Thankfully I've been married to an absolute angel of a woman for over twenty years, and I've learned to trust her intuition. I investigate more closely when Mandy says something is amiss.

I've also benefited greatly from the spiritual sensitivity of other believers as they've said things like, "I don't have a peace about that." Even when they can't put it into words, there is a mysterious discernment at play. The reality is that we all run the risk of foolishly trusting our instincts, even my sweetie.

Many an angry blog post begins with someone saying that something just felt "off." But that's not their *introduction* to the cold hard facts. Those *are* their cold hard facts. The rationale is that something *is off* whenever something *feels off.*

Period.

The preaching felt off.
The doctrine felt off.
The leader felt off.
The culture felt off.

Jeremiah reminds us in the seventeenth chapter that our hearts are deceitful, and sick, and hard to understand. Our intuition can be frail, desperate, and manipulative, so wisdom admits that we're not always right.

# My Truth

Modernism contends that there is a truth, and that humanity desires to go and find it. Truth is huddled up on some mountain, or in the center of the universe, or renting space in the choir loft, but for the modernists, truth is tangible and is someplace on the proverbial map.

For the postmodern thinker, truth is not central, but instead, truths are out there, and we just pick our favorites like we're celebrating Granny's 80th at Golden Corral.

Truth is a buffet, and we're all picky eaters.

Somewhat shamefully, we all head to our seats with a small salad and a meat plate that tears the rotator cuff—just me?

Some of us didn't fan the plate temperature down, so now our Jell-O square is melting and gliding 62 miles per hour across the plate, threatening our church shoes.

We find ourselves more and more in a world of critical-realistic thought as opposed to the modern and postmodern worlds. This framework contends that truth cannot be found, nor do we need to pick and choose truth. Instead, we're the chef. We cook up our own truth. We decide what truth we want to live with. Like an Instagram feed, we unfollow and like so as to paint the walls of our personal universe just the right shade. We become authors and editors of our own truth.

"Lying should be celebrated as creativity."
"Open marriage is marriage."
"*My Jesus* has blue eyes."
"Front-porch lemonade is 'Christ' to me."

I think of Oprah saying something like, "If people felt free to be themselves and follow their passions, the world would be a better place." Oprah didn't broadcast her well-intentioned self-help from a crack house in Chicago. No, she'd moved from Chicago to Hollywood and was shooting the episode from her remote garden with West Elm padded yard furniture and armed security at the gate.

You see, it's easy for Oprah to live according to her truth, because the ugly reality out there is easier to ignore with that much money, and a few Glocks in her security team's holsters.

**Culture tells us that truth is a matter of personal preference.**

So, if we're not looking, this sort of truth framework can cause us to approach our faith with ourselves in mind.

Our minds on ourselves.
Minding ourselves.

We begin to curate our own spiritual universe, like a word salad; hold the tomatoes.

Proof text here.

Half text there.

Preference here.

Avoidance there.

Ah, just the way I like it.

Goldilocks and her golden rule.

It's not uncommon to hear, "God's love really works for me, but the whole hell thing is just a bit barbaric" or "I'm not super into the Old Testament" or "I'd fast, but I just have some health challenges… like hunger, headache, weight loss, and chronic hangriness…"

It's easy to imagine how this sort of approach causes the modern struggling Christian to resist a universe of reason by creating their own spiritual world.

The backbeat of the whole dance thumps of individualism.

Me.

My needs.

My truth.

I used to believe that lawmakers understood the dangers of individualism better than most because legislation has two primary effects. It affects people today through today's bill. But more importantly, it affects all people tomorrow as it sets precedence for legislation going forward.

What's allowed today will justify what's allowed tomorrow.
What is normalized today will determine where the frontier starts, and thus what is to be conquered next.

Some call it a slippery slope, some call it progress, and some call it irresponsible.
"How will this affect those around me?" That is the principle oft-forgotten in a "choose my own reality" pseudo-reality.

Please remember that sin is never siloed.

Sin is watercolor.

Those pencil lines don't stand a chance of containing it.

Not only do my actions affect others.

My ideas affect others.

My ideas influence others' ideas.

And my ideas influence my actions.

I write with fear. Not just fear of what I say or don't say, but fear of what you think I'm saying, and fear of what sort of foundation I'm laying for others to build upon.

# Check Yourself

Culture celebrates certainty.

I know, that doesn't feel true at first blush, but stroll with me.
No one celebrates the gullible.

We celebrate the well-read, the data-informed, the critical thinkers. Hume and Locke have led us to live like our five senses are
our most trusted advisors. Empiricism is the emperor, and those
peasants of intuition, emotion, and wonder had better grab their

hay brooms and scurry back to their awkward little shacks out of view. Because materialism, "just can't with them."

When certainty is the gold standard of faith, then we can't believe at all if we're not certain of it all. And once we have made certain that we do not believe, we are certain, beyond all doubt, that we don't believe, and that believing is certainly out of the question. Dizzy yet?

Follow this.
Some rebel against heavy-handed church cultures of doctrinal certainty, only to adopt an equally toxic deconstructionist certainty.

When I scroll through the horn options and light shows in my friend Matt's Tesla, I'm so grateful for the life provided me by trusting things I don't understand. I seriously don't understand how they cram all that tech in there, but it did help to hear someone say it's a glorified iPhone that can actually get you to work.

Certainty is a sturdy house, but its walls are closing in.
And I can sense you nodding along with my words.
So now that I've won you over, I'll flip the coin.

# In Dig Nation

Currently, people are paying to destroy old TVs and play T-ball with plates in rage rooms. Not a bad business. Put broken appliances and worthless glassware in warehouse spaces with baseball bats and axes, then charge people by the minute. It sounds fun.

It sounds a bit like our cultural moment.

Indignation is now the resting face of those who "care about the world."

**Culture celebrates rage, and for many, faith is in its crosshairs.**

Empowerment is rarely framed as an opportunity to think through a measured response. Empowerment is often a call to arms. Culture's call to speak up is disproportionate to its call to listen.

My wife and I have been flipping houses for some time, and true to DIY TV wisdom, demo day is fun. You know what's not fun? Crown molding day and carpet the stairs day. On the day of the open house, it's comforting to prospective home buyers to say that you've "taken it down to the studs." Ripping everything out, especially the kitchen sink, is often the ticket to money-town.

Listen, demo day takes brute force, but it also takes vision. We use spray paint and put huge Xs on walls that have got to go, and if Jeff is helping, we go over the boundaries an extra time because he's the deacon of destruction and he's darn good at it.

If I'm smart on demo day, I have destruction on my mind but open house in my heart. I must see past demo day. I must not find my joy in the rage of demo day. Instead, my joy is in the rebuild.

Jacques Derrida, the father of deconstruction, was criticized by his contemporaries for his never-ending demo day. Cambridge University sought to give him an honorary degree in the early '90s, but many said that his work boiled down to "foolish, half-hearted blows to the value of reason, truth, and scholarship." NEEDS CITATION Maybe *The Times* (London). Saturday, May 9, 1992

When I engage with those who demolish, I must ask myself, "What have they built?"

The open house justifies demo day. You won't last long in the biz if you're quite good at demo day but hold no open houses.

You'll be upside down in your ideas.

───────

I love watching young kids play in the sandbox as long as there are no neighborhood cats. I love seeing them get just the right water to sand ratio and create bucket-shaped buildings, but I smile really big when I hear the sounds of destruction cross their lips as they grab the vintage metal toy truck to bring it all down. It's cute and virtually harmless because sandcastles lose no value when flattened. Child's play is just that.

My tour guide in Israel told the group that Israel's largest budget item is its air force, and its second greatest expense is archaeology. They're discovering and preserving history both large and small, all over the country. It's fascinating to look at artifacts, from those as small as a "widow's mite" coin, to whole cities with first-century Roman spas. You can see ornate mosaic floors lined up on a main street from the time of Jesus. They're beautifully laid in twenty-foot sections, each the remains of a different business.

For excavation and preservation, one must dig, but dig carefully.
One must disrupt with reverence.
The archaeologist does not rage, but searches.
Your faith is worth an orderly mess.

Your faith is not worthless sand; it is the pearl of great price. Our faith is museum-worthy, and perhaps it's forty feet deep, covered over by hurt, confusion, ego, and man-made religion. But take it slow.

Don't *vroom* your faith.
Find an air hose and a tiny brush.
You'd sure hate to run a hole through a priceless treasure.

Less sandbox rage, more museum rigor.

Rage has the force of an atomic bomb, but restraint has the strength of the Hoover Dam. Hoover's walls are two football fields thick, and its impact is massive. Over 18 million people in Los Angeles, Las Vegas, and San Diego rely on the dam for water. Prior to its completion, downstream settlement was impossible due to seasonal flooding. Now, Hoover's restraint provides power for some in Nevada, Arizona, and California.

Even those rage room operators acknowledge the reality that so few do. Rage is dangerous. They take great care to get guests to sign waivers and wear gloves, helmets, and eye protection. They prohibit customers from clobbering other guests, and they won't let you bring the bat into the reception area. Perhaps this fevered rage has led to a growing number of people sharing the brewing conviction that we live in an inescapable battle between race, gender, and phobia.

———

It's not uncommon for my wife to offer to clean my glasses for me, and when she does, it's a whole new world. Dazzling, shimmering, new horizons! Lenses have a profound effect on what you see.

Whether it's sunglasses at the beach or a new prescription, what you're looking through matters. I'm concerned that the family of

God might wear their mainstream cultural conflict glasses into church, and they're not even those snazzy transition lenses.

Humans have a way of finding what they're looking for.

I once fielded a critique that our church didn't trust women to lead.
What supporting evidence was offered?
Wait for it.

Oddly, the evidence was that we had women leading in every area of ministry since day one. Yeah. For this person, having women in leadership was a smoke-screen hiding the fact that we didn't trust women to lead.

We have a way of finding what we're looking for, don't we?

Christian unity must make no room for prejudice in any form. I say this with the utmost conviction. May God root out any foul racist, sexist, or phobic pride from my heart and the hearts of His people. Some flocks have been the worst of offenders, some still are, and our church is still in process. With that said, culture has emboldened God's people to bring toxic assumptions and lenses to family reunions, and many are finding just what they knew they'd find.

The VA has spent no small amount of money researching the psychology behind combat addiction. Some soldiers just can't settle back into civilian life.

The adrenaline.
The fame.
The fraternity.
The mission.
The structure.
The pace.

Peacetime is bland by comparison, and for many mental-health professionals, this rage addiction is classified as disordered. This is not healthy.

Could it be that our culture wars, along with news networks that offer nightly boot camp, have led to the army of God incessantly fidgeting in the pews?

# Twins/Friends

There's an old-school church proverb that says, "Hate the sin, love the sinner." We live in a day and age that tells me that in order to love someone, I must also approve of all their behaviors and share their exact convictions.

If I don't, I'm a bigot.
If I don't, I'm narrow-minded.
If I don't, I'm unloving.

When this belief takes root in the heart of a believer, there's little to no value in confession, accountability, reasoned debate, or any concrete discussion of sin or sanctification.

Culture seems to think that love must never disagree.
Culture says we must be twins to be friends.

I have hope that behind closed doors, people are hypocrites. My hunch is that those who say these things don't actually live these things. I hope that accepting and affirming parents still tell their kids to pick up their shoes. They don't accept slobbish behavior or affirm a cleaning strike. My hope is that those who say love is love don't still sleep with their sister or their neighbor's wife. I hope those who speak of "my truth" don't hand their keys to the first person who lays claim to their car. For their own sake, I hope anarchists still lock their doors at night.

Loud movements are often shallow.
Volume instead of texture.

Red-faced passion instead of compelling raised eyebrows.

Crack houses buzz with acceptance and welcome, especially if you bring a rock or two. If you're highly allergic to tension, then a convicting sermon is dangerous and unloving. This sort of approach also requires great creativity and effort to reframe Christian ethics in a less concrete way. If true Christ-like love is to endorse every person's reading of the scriptures, then the Good Book is boiled to death. And we all know that if you leave the pot to boil too long, there'll be nothing left of it.

The living water can evaporate into thick air.

It would be fair to speculate, under this dogma, that to be the most loving person in the room, one must have no convictions about right or wrong.

May I suggest that love must disagree?

Disagreement and standards are the building blocks of development, healthy life choices, and purification. It's true in sports, business, and character development.

True friends are able to keep an even keel, even when at odds.

# Just You Wait, Buddy

I am so grateful for progress.

I dream more than I reminisce.

I see a bright road ahead.


Clean water flows more than ever. Communication across languages and distance is faster than ever. Women are voting; smallpox is like quicksand, fabled at this point. Cancer treatment is improving. So in many respects, we're living in the most privileged time in history, but if we're not careful, we'll mistake every development that comes along as healthy and inevitable.

There can be an almost fairy-tale quality to the future, as though the future is always right. If you don't shift with the majority, then you are to be pitied. From this understanding, there can be great fear of being on the wrong side of history.

Matthew, in the seventh chapter of his Gospel, recounts a time when Jesus said He was like a narrow gate and that many would not squeeze through Him, but instead would walk toward destruction, like a parade. He then said that few would walk toward life.

My point is that disagreeing with the majority is not inherently immoral.

Jesus and pop culture will never duet well, and at times, it's painfully bad jazz.

**In different ways, culture foolishly tells us that their take on the future is right, and seeks to convince us that being on the wrong side of history is worse than death.**

"This is where we're headed, and if you don't align, you're going to regret it."

I've caught myself trying to be God's public relations department to somehow make peace with where I felt the majority was headed. I was trying to make certain that Jesus didn't end up on the wrong side of history, but that was a fool's errand. Regrettably, I've strutted out to that podium to negotiate a peace deal between God and popular opinion.

On my clearest days, I'm more concerned about being on the right side of God than I am being on the right side of history.

There was a time when those who said that pornography would deeply wound humanity were on the wrong side of history. People laughed. There are pockets of the world where the laughter is turning to slow, regretful groans. Those on the wrong side of history are now seen as those who are on the right side of history, as the poisoned fruit of porn is rotting on the vine.

The church martyrs seemed to agree that neither the future nor history are LORD, and it cost them their heads.

# 5 HOW TO STOP THE BLEEDING: A WAY FORWARD FOR YOU AND YOUR CHURCH

**Maybe you're reading this because you are in a faith crisis.**


Thanks for reading this far.


Maybe you're reading this to better serve a friend who's going through it.
Thanks for your commitment to discipleship and helping others follow Jesus in real time.


Perhaps you're a pastor.

I'm grateful for your time.

No matter your role, let's finish by talking about what we can do to better serve those who are in this critical season. May God give you grace to know how to proceed, especially if you're in the pew and not the pastorate.

## 1. Normalize uncertainty.

Refuse to be satisfied with just giving the "right" answer. If you suspect it's a pat answer or has no sincere footing, continue to seek the honest answer.

Perhaps your children's ministry wants to spend a few minutes enhancing its lessons to bring fullness to their otherwise flat stories. Make room for fullness.

If it remains taboo to ask for clarity at a women's table discussion, you might end up with a church full of Bible bees but no honey in the hive—no sweetness of the Spirit working on the inside. Encourage questions.

At least some of our faith must be built upon personal experience.

Are there opportunities in your church for people to practice depending on God? Maybe it's a risky outreach, or a mission trip, or a big financial goal that you are believing for, together. It's easy to outgrow faith if it remains infantile or second-hand. Let's fill a landfill with our spiritual onesies.

Where would you like your church to build in a bit of risk and uncertainty?

## 2. Triage the hurt.

Triage is a medical term that, in part, deals with the need to treat every wound in a swift and appropriate manner. It organizes resources and staff to deal with suffering in the most efficient way possible.

Perhaps it's time to invite people to talk about their church hurt. I know that sounds crazy!

It seems easier to maintain a "don't ask, don't tell" policy. But I assure you that the hurt is under the surface, like the lava under Barren Island.

Are your pastors in the habit of looking for it, or are they oblivious to the pain in the bones of the sheep? They might be frustrated by the pace of the flock if they're unaware of the trauma's arthritic effect.

Are the small-group leaders at your church trained to support the wounded?

Is your church board willing to pay for a trusted and godly therapist to step in when needed?

What safeguards are in place to guard against sexual harassment, bullying, and bitterness?

Do the youth ministry leaders ride in cars alone with students?
Are there safeguards from working volunteers too much?
Is there a ministry that fields concerns from people in the church?
Are investigations done by third parties when allegations are brought?

Are there times when true abuse is dismissed as "enemy attacks" or somehow downplayed through church jargon?

### 3. Schedule contentious content.

I'd suggest your church create goals that facilitate speaking about hard things with some regularity. Goals are only as helpful as they are measurable. Perhaps you'd like to post twice a year calling out racism. Maybe it'd be helpful to preach once a quarter about the ugly side of church. Maybe it makes sense to run a six-week course on God's sexual ethic. If we're not intentional, we'll avoid difficult subjects and realities. Clear and measurable goals will help us create the healthy culture we desire.

Make a list of topics.
Put them on the calendar.

When political issues are on everyone's mind, dig deep to elevate Jesus as the central focus of His church, and celebrate the godly motivations that influence each side. Do not alienate one side of the church to appease the other.

Help your church equip your small-group leaders to navigate tension.

Remind the leaders around you that there will always be people on their team who vote differently, and encourage them to be mindful not to speak flippantly in a way that shames people for landing somewhere different than those around them.

Have you ever noticed how strangers are rarely forgiven or given the chance to change? Strangers are easily written off. But when your friend flies off the handle, you walk through it together, and you both grow. We need more friends and fewer strangers in our faith communities. Consider picnics, game nights, and inviting a few potential friends over for dinner. (Just not on election night; we don't need to go too crazy!) Creating opportunities for relationships to grow and for people to meet new friends helps to combat the assumption that churches are full of hypocrites.

### 4. Minister presence.

Given that we have big feelings in crises, and we often adopt big convictions in crises, the church must work earnestly to ensure that people are cared for well when things are hard.

Perhaps the pastor is great at hospital visits, or maybe someone on staff is the empathetic voice, or maybe there's the expectation that small-group leaders are the first touch point for visitors.

I was both shocked and blessed when my dear friend Jenni told me that she *loves* walking with people through dark seasons. I had never imagined that someone enjoyed that. But she does, and she is the Jordan of grief ministry.

How does your church guard against people being forgotten? Is it working? Trust me on this one: every church has shepherding blind spots. We continue to struggle and grow in this area.

## 5. Exercise the whole body.

Every church should seek to worship God with their heads, hearts, and hands.

Reason.
Passion.
Work.

Or maybe it's thinking, feeling, and doing.

Regardless of how you frame it, every church naturally gravitates to one manner of engagement over others, and by default, every church lacks in one area more than others. What sorts of metrics do you want to use to try to speak to all three sorts of disciples?

Speak to the whole body.

We are the body of Christ, and every member is essential, but if we're not careful, our churches will settle on a strategy that fixates on the new person so much that the rooted members are forgotten.

How does your church meet the needs of the faithful? Are there opportunities for deeper study? Are there sermons that go beyond introductory truths? Do we publicly celebrate constancy, punctuality, and tenure?

Don't forget the faithful.

How can your church be gracious to the flaky while making sure they understand that they're missing out on so much?

It's loving to tell the truth about consistency.
Perhaps your church's unending welcome encourages inconsistent attendance and is keeping people from the powerful effects of coming together often!

So, call your friend when they miss, celebrate the in-person gathering on social media, and pick them up when they need a ride.

In order to combat nominal Christianity, you might consider having attendance requirements for some small groups. While I admit that grace and understanding have their place, there's also a place for expectation and priority setting.

It's a bit of an oversimplification, but the primary difference between propagation and inoculation is volume. Vaccines have just enough virus to build immunity; a full-on dose would give you the real thing. Some people are inoculated to the power of the gospel and the power of church community.

## 6. Unmask the church's structure.

I once had a business owner ask for a meeting. Once we settled in, he asked for a church organizational chart, then a decision flow chart, then a mission statement, and then some governing values. He then asked politely for a high-level general budget rundown. These simple explanations and particulars provided him the security he needed to confidently jump in.

It got me thinking about trust.

The more nebulous the church, the longer it takes to trust the church.

Given that many come with a basic distrust of organizations and leaders, how clear is the organizational side of your church?

Does your church need name tags?
Does your church need a staff page?
How often does your church have a business meeting?
Do people know who the elders are?
Is your church transparent with its finances?

You don't have to podcast long to find churches referred to as families. Rarely do pastors speak of the assembly as a business, but the truth is that every church must do business like every family must do business. They must pay their bills, have a household budget, live within their means, save, risk, and learn to be generous. Does your congregation seem to be bashful about the business dealings of the church? They shouldn't be. Many a house falls due to financial neglect, and just like marriage, the most loving and fruitful conversations often happen on *Money Mondays*; just ask Dave.

## 7. Don't frustrate the friendships.

Just after I'd ironed out the ground rules with my tablemates in the fourth grade, Mrs. Dyer rearranged the seating chart. Now I was sitting in a circle with all new tablemates. By nature, I love change. But even so, the effects of the change were noticeable. The culture of our table was impacted by which of us hoodlums were sitting at it. Which clown stirred up the clowning? It was different every day.

This interconnected, highly relational web provides an ever-changing environment for growth. As humans rub shoulders, we must learn how to create peace, how to be patient, how to be self-controlled, and how to forgive.

I think church should look a bit more like my fourth-grade pod than a college lecture in the auditorium where we shuffle in, sit down, listen, and leave.

My pastor Jim taught me that the church exists to make disciples: those who are saved by Jesus, changed by Jesus, and on mission with Jesus.

The mission of Jesus is to employ every believer to personally help someone else follow Him. Hopefully, lots of someones over the course of a believer's life!

I'm convinced that the greatest way to help people follow Jesus in real time is to actually know them.

What lies do they tend to live by?

What gifts are they developing?

What support would be most helpful as they mature?

Relationships are indispensable in Jesus' mission.

Curriculum can't replace relationships.

Bigger worship centers can't replace relationships.

Better preaching can't replace them.

Dreamy worship bands can't replace them.

Slogans, banners, and creative storytelling can't replace relationships.

If this is true, then we'd be wise to bend our church programs and our schedules around this relational reality. Get to church early. Take people to coffee. Actually answer your phone. Our finances must reflect it, and even our homes and church buildings must work to create an atmosphere conducive to personal connection.

Perhaps there should be fewer pews and more coffee tables because, often, heartfelt conversations can handle questions and bring clarification in a way that preaching and doctrinal statements can't.

Create small groups!

Get into a small group.

Never miss your small group.

Make sure to prioritize the relationships within your small group.

Hear me out.

It's easy to leave something you think is monolithic, especially if you wrongly assume everyone believes that one thing you're campaigning against. But small groups allow people to see the variety within the church. For instance, four people will read a passage and it will be applied four different ways as the Holy Spirit mysteriously leads. This variety has a way of guarding us from our erroneous assumptions about the church. It takes the wind out of the skeptic's sail.

**8. Create a robust support of the Bible.**

It's one thing to offer biblical support for a position, but what deliberate support does your church offer for its position on the Bible?

Why do you trust the Bible?
Have you grown in your understanding lately?
Why does your church study, preach, teach, and build upon the Bible? This is a good question for both church leaders and members.

If your church builds everything on the authority of scripture, then it's got to do some work helping people understand why the scriptures can be trusted.

Where do you present evidence of the Bible's archaeological accuracy? Are you ready to answer those sorts of questions from your kids or neighbors?

Where does your church help people understand the Bible's canonization? Have you ever heard of the Dead Sea Scrolls?

Would you like to pull Pliny the Younger or Tacitus into the equation and show how first-century contemporary historians offer extra-biblical support for the claims of the New Testament?

Maybe we want to hold seminars that dive deeply into topics or books of the Bible.

It might be helpful for the church to create an annual report of sorts—something that shows what scriptures were taught on Sundays, studied in Bible study, covered in kids' church, and discussed in small groups. If you find your list is thin, then widen it.

My gut tells me quite a few of our "Bible problems" would vanish if we spent a bit more time employing apologetic and historical material to back up our high view of the scriptures.

## 9. Lower the stage.

Most leaders figure out that whatever they celebrate will be replicated.
It's human nature to tend to do the activity that is regularly applauded.

It's easy for me to imagine a world in which your pastor spends an extra six hours in his study to craft the zinger that'll bring another "Great word!" and a handshake on Sunday morning, but what would happen if your pastor showed up without a sermon next week because he had spent a great number of hours slowly walking with a church member through the valley of doubt?

What if your church lowered the stage metaphorically?

What if your leaders felt well-equipped and encouraged to take their time doing the same thing? What if fruitfulness was measured in patience with new Christians, not just performance in corporate worship?

How do you feel when things aren't quite as sharp because discipleship takes time?

My grandfather colorfully communicated to his pastor that he needed to slow down when he walked through the church foyer. He was preaching *at* them in the sanctuary, then ignoring them in the foyer. The exchange involved a curse word, and a nearly dislocated shoulder as he yanked the young pastor aside, but it left an impression on the preacher. It also impacted me when I heard the grateful pastor tell the story at my grandpa's funeral.

Sometimes we all need an old man to remind us that Instant Pots taste different than the simmer does.

It might do us some good to think of the family of God more like an airline than an Olympic runner. Arriving number one is not as important as arriving in one piece.

## 10. Embrace the peculiar.

When preachers talk shop, they say things like, "Get your Bible and a newspaper, open them up on your desk, and write yourself a banger of a sermon!" or "You gotta speak to people's Mondays, not just their Sundays!"

"Give 'em heaven, but don't forget they are made out of earth!"

It takes some skill and a whimsical melody to marry application and revelation, but at some point, every church must help people think about current events by actually talking about current events.

I've heard of churches creating current events classes. I've heard of churches using a prayer time in service to address current events or putting current events into their regular social media rotation. Whatever you do, there's got to be a sense that we are a peculiar people and that cultural conflict is to be a normal part of the believer's life.

Within a few months of following Jesus, new believers in your church should have the sense that they are altogether different from the world. There should be a growing sense that the world's values and cravings don't fit any longer. It should feel as if they've outgrown them, as if their hearts have been renovated down to the studs.

Remember this when you're helping someone follow Jesus in real time. Remember this at your dinner table. Remember this if you make church-wide decisions.

**11. Major in majors, minor in minors, and define the two.**

The supremacy of Jesus is quite an important conviction for those within the Christian faith. What you do with Harry Potter is not. It would be helpful to come up with a clear list of close-handed issues and open-handed issues in your church. It might be a fruitful exercise to start putting together your own personal list.

Where would a church member look to find the non-negotiable teachings of the church? And for extra credit, would they be able to find a list of a few open-handed or debatable issues somewhere?

Where might your church present this sort of information?

Do people know that there are tongue-talkers on staff?

Has it been revealed that your youth pastor doesn't believe in the "Left Behind" rapture?

Is it okay to disagree about the state of the dead?

Robust debates surrounding nonessential theological positions are some of the greatest faith-enhancing conversations to which a growing Christian can be exposed. But what if the boundaries are so vague that it's dangerous for them to engage because they won't know when their ship has left orthodoxy?

## 12. Give curiosity a budget line.

There's a specific phrase my kids are sick of hearing. It's a phrase I've gleefully given when asked about house projects they want done or family vacations they want to take. It's a phrase they've heard too many times, and they're organizing and it's getting dangerous.

"All it takes is time and money," I say.

Orren, my wise-bulldog youngest son snickers. He gets me and my humor.

His siblings clench their fists. I can see it. They're tempted to think ungodly thoughts *at* me.

But I'm right.

When we look at our churches, we must ask, "What time and money have been allocated to create venues that accommodate questions, emotions, and objections?"

Think those through.

Questions.
Emotions.
Objections.

Those are three interruptions to the standard sermon. And for good reason, as sermons aren't meant to accommodate them.

Was the counselor's salary spent on the LED wall?
Would your men's pastor rather preach another forty minutes or break up into groups?
Is your family schedule so crunched for time that there's never

time for questions or objections? I'm not exactly advocating for a Sunday-morning free-for-all, but there must be some smaller groups that lean toward dialogue as opposed to monologue.

I'm regularly taken aback with how environment shapes behavior. Are there quiet meetings that make it easy to ponder, or are they all high-energy and celebratory?

Do the kids ever leave the room so that their parents can share about their marital struggles?

Are there leaders who ask twice for objections and then hug the objector as they leave the house?

If you designed some environments differently, you just might find that your friends show a different side of themselves.

## 13. Be approachable.

I know. Your church sings that one pseudo-secular song every Sunday to meet non-Christians where they are, but I'm wondering if the average person feels welcomed to voice a concern when they have one. An open door might be just the innovation we need.

The open door helps us to meet them where they are, because they'll take all the guesswork out of it as they reveal their questions and hangups.

Do we come off as defensive, or are we open to feedback?

Never hesitate to humble yourself as a church, as both leaders and members. If you model repentance, growth, and mutual submission, I'm certain the enemy's lies about your having a controlling spirit just won't land.

Is it legal for the preacher to correct their own sermon from last week?

Is it okay for the church staff to say, "We thought that would work, but it didn't"?

How much time do we spend covering up when we should be fessing up?

Do staff members know that failure is not automatic grounds for dismissal? What if confessing a porn habit didn't get them canned? Wouldn't it be great if the church's reputation was one of transparency and teachability?

## 14. Celebrate honest diversity.

My friend Jeff asked me years ago, "Why don't Black people come to this church?"

After some thought, I answered, "Because nobody wants to be the first."

It was an overly simplistic response, but it holds some truth. We naturally connect to environments where we see reflections of ourselves. Whether it's age, race, tenure, style, profession, or status, we look, to some degree, for people like us.

In what ways can your church highlight the variety in its fold?

Please don't scour the internet for multicultural photos and plaster them all over the walls.

Your church is diverse; it just might take a new prescription to see it.

Do you celebrate leaders?

How about the followers around you?

How about the feelers, empaths, penny pinchers, Excel lovers, huggers, or flighty types?

Is your church Instagram monochromatic?

Are only "cool" people allowed on stage?

Where's that B3 organ? The old folks might miss it!

Does the liberal ever preach?
How about the more conservative elder?
Are women essential when making decisions?

When was the last time your church utilized a panel discussion in youth group?

Or is it just the man or woman of God bringing a word from God, to the people of God, to be honored by God, and treated like they themselves are God? That was a tad extreme, but you get the point. What if an unbeliever was asked to share their observations of the text in a seminar? How might that change the atmosphere?

Jesus said that the Pharisees made people in their own image: "sons of hell." I'll take it a step further and say that hell rejoices when leaders seek only to make "mini-mes"—carbon copies of themselves—instead of seeking to see all sorts of folks developed into incredibly redeemed expressions of God's creativity with their own combination of gifts, talents, passions, and abilities.

## one final plea

As the church turns her face to the horizon, we have great reason to bask in the golden glow. It's been a long day, but our faith—even with all its blemishes and troubles—is nothing to be embarrassed about.

The ways of Jesus are sound.
And the Bride of Christ is poised to win.

The poor footings will sink, culture's walls will crack, and the lies will topple in a great crash. But the foundation of Christ Jesus will support His church. We'll still need a dumpster from time to time, but we'll continue to build with care, because the family of God needs a house as we await our eternal home.

The reward will be great.

The great builder will smile, faith will become sight, and the church will gasp at all He's gone on to prepare for Her.

# Acknowledgments

Kansas City's Nelson Art Gallery has the most gigantic badminton birdie sculptures on their perfectly groomed lawn. Eighteen feet, and over two tons of quirky, striking, and perfectly ill-placed goodness! If I were to see them in the back of a garage, or at the junkyard, I would wince, but their placement seems to set the scene perfectly. I am one of these.

My wife, Mandy, has given so much to set me up for success. Without her artistic eye, my insecurities, lack of discipline, and the hustle of life would have bossed me around, and this book wouldn't exist. She has a way of casting me in just the right light and cheering me on.

I'm grateful for my children's commitment to our family and their passion for Jesus. I also benefit greatly from the fact that they don't tell all the stories they could about me. There's a genuine sense of peace and margin needed to write a book, and their maturity and love for life have made that margin possible for me. I am grateful.

Steve saw me in the corner of a barn someplace and dared to bring me out, dust me off, and committed to getting me as presentable as possible. He has coached me. He has forgiven me. He has defended me, and he has just been *there* with me through so so much.

Many thanks to Mandy, Steve, Sean, Jeni, Lance, Kathy, Brandon, and Jason for all their commas, rebukes, additions, and subtractions to this manuscript. This book is far better due to your investments.

Perhaps the largest part of the proverbial museum lawn is our church. Greenhouse Church has been a safe place to explore these and other complex issues. They've granted me time off to write (thanks, Pastor Sean, for preaching all summer) and the ability to be a human in process, learning, growing, getting it wrong many times, and getting it painfully right, once. It takes a lot of grace, faith, and loyalty to get me to look like anything resembling art, so I'm grateful for all the risk-taking artists aforementioned. So here I rest. Quirky. Striking. And perfectly ill-placed. I am rich in friends.